SUSAN GELT

THE
NEW
WOMEN'S MOVEMENT

RESTORING OUR POSITION.
RECLAIMING OUR POWER.

THE NEW WOMEN'S MOVEMENT

Copyright © 2017—Susan Gelt-Garcia

First Print

All rights reserved. This book is protected by the copyright laws of the United States of America. This book may not be copied or reprinted for commercial gain or profit. Permission will be granted upon request.

Holy Bible, New Living Translation, copyright © 1996, 2004, 2015 by Tyndale House Foundation. Used by permission of Tyndale House Publishers Inc., Carol Stream, Illinois 60188. All rights reserved.

Scripture taken from the NEW AMERICAN STANDARD BIBLE®, Copyright © 1960,1962,1 963,1968,1971,1972,1973,1975,1977,1995 by The Lockman Foundation. Used by permission.

The Living Bible copyright © 1971 by Tyndale House Foundation. Used by permission of Tyndale House Publishers Inc., Carol Stream, Illinois 60188. All rights reserved.

Scripture taken from the New King James Version®. Copyright © 1982 by Thomas Nelson. Used by permission. All rights reserved.

Copyright © 2015 by The Lockman Foundation, La Habra, CA 90631. All rights reserved.

THE HOLY BIBLE, NEW INTERNATIONAL VERSION®, NIV® Copyright © 1973, 1978, 1984, 2011 by Biblica, Inc.® Used by permission. All rights reserved worldwide.

The ESV® Bible (The Holy Bible, English Standard Version®). ESV® Permanent Text Edition® (2016). Copyright © 2001 by Crossway, a publishing ministry of Good News Publishers. The ESV® text has been reproduced in cooperation with and by permission of Good News Publishers. Unauthorized reproduction of this publication is prohibited. All rights reserved.

The Holy Bible: International Standard Version. Release 2.0, Build 2015.02.09. Copyright © 1995-2014 by ISV Foundation. ALL RIGHTS RESERVED INTERNATIONALLY. Used by permission of Davidson Press, LLC.

Scripture taken from The Message. Copyright © 1993, 1994, 1995, 1996, 2000, 2001, 2002. Used by permission of NavPress Publishing Group.

Cover by Brianna Ailie I www.briannaailie.com
Interior by A.B.[Banales]
Picture of Susan Gelt taken by LaNette Harding

ISBN: 978-1-94650303-9

Printed in the United States

SUSAN GELT-GARCIA

THE
NEW
WOMEN'S MOVEMENT

RESTORING OUR POSITION.
RECLAIMING OUR POWER.

TABLE OF CONTENTS

Foreword	vii
A Very Important Preface	ix
Introduction	xiii
1 ‖ We Were Created to Encompass	1
2 ‖ Encompasser, the Original Design of Woman	25
3 ‖ The Fall of Mankind	43
4 ‖ The Corrupt Pattern: Women Intensely Crave and Men Rule Over	67
5 ‖ The Path to Restoration	93
6 ‖ When Women Encompass	121
7 ‖ The Big Picture	149
One Last Word	173
Notes	183

FOREWORD

By Pastor Patrick Sparrow
Equippers Church of the Central Coast

There has been a progressive heavenly download coming into the hearts of Kingdom Influencers to "wash" the Body of Christ with a revelation of Kingdom identity. The fundamental understanding of how God made us and why God made us has the profound power to transform people from victim to victor, from pauper to royalty, from inconsequential to radical leader. Susan's book *The New Women's Movement* is a heavenly download and has the spiritual DNA to be catalytic in transforming people unto a new and eternal identity. This awakens their relationship with God as well as realigns other key relationships, especially marriage.

My wife, Terri, and I have been friends and pastors to Susan for several years. We have seen the special effect of grace through her life as she leads Women Ministries and teaches and preaches the Word. This work of authorship is not a product of soulish searching and study but rather a spiritual collection of revelations that she has gleaned from her journey with the Lord, inspired by great times of joy as well as great times of suffering.

THE NEW WOMEN'S MOVEMENT

As a reader I encourage you to meditate on these things, sometimes forgetting traditional thoughts and teachings, looking afresh into the Word of God, asking the Holy Spirit to lead into the truth bearing witness of new freedom, a new time, and a new movement.

A VERY IMPORTANT PREFACE

This book is a call to all women, young and old, married or single, and in every culture:

You are not below or beneath. You are not an afterthought. Woman was not created as an assistant to help man in his important call nor were you created to assuage his loneliness. You were created as a valuable part of a two-part leadership team. For those of you who are married, your two-part leadership team is also to function as one-flesh interdependent leaders, and together, as one flesh, you reflect the image of the triune God, and were called to rule and reign over planet Earth.

Your important contribution to this two-part leadership team is the valuable supply of your perceptions, insights, and all you have sensed through your connection to the Spirit of God. Your part is to create atmosphere and to release the flow of the Spirit of God outward. You are His anointed daughter, and it is not His desire that you be diminished or devalued. You are valuable and beautiful and loved and powerful.

God wants to work through you to reflect His image and His glory on Earth. He wants you to use the unique gifts and abilities He put inside you, as you partner with others in taking dominion over the planet and releasing His Power. He wants you to function as the powerful woman He created you to be: sensitive, intuitive, and, like the Holy Spirit, empowered and enabled to live in the realm of the spirit and of the soul (the world of feelings and impressions and sensitivities). This is you at your best, how you were created to function.

He wants you, all of you. He wants a deep love relationship with you. You belong to God as His daughter and His wife. In the intimacy of those relationships, all your needs are met. He is your good father and your perfect husband. He wants to lavish love upon you, unashamedly and without reservation. He wants to love on you every day and intimately live life with you, at your side, continually.

As you grow in your ability to stay in His presence and connected to Him, you can create and maintain a powerful circle of life over your relationships, a circuit of life energy that is the flow of the Spirit of God. From that circuit, your husband or if you are single, to some degree, the men in your life will discover a greater ability to function in the perfect, original design that God has for them. For the married women: as you encompass your husband he will flow back into you, in the rhythm and design in which you were created to function. In this flow of movement, the two opposite but equal parts of man and woman become one flesh. The two become one and enjoy intimate communion with each other and the Lord. He created you to function together as one, and in that you are blessed, blessed beyond measure. For the single women: you can influence the men in your life, too. You can find peaceful connections and better relationships with these men and they can benefit from the powerful position you were designed for. All of you can carry God's heart to mankind and extend His rule over the planet.

It is time to return to that place, to return to that position. It is time for your original design to be restored to who you were created to be, a valuable and important leader and influencer of mankind. As you return to that position, single women will find peaceful completion in their singleness. Married women will find rest; their marriages can be restored to His original one-flesh design. Hurting women and unhealthy marriages can find help and healing. No matter the depth of your hurt or the lack thereof, this book will bring you greater understanding. You can and you will truly walk in the power to create, dominate evil, rule over the Earth, solve the problems of today, and prosper in all of your life. You will rule, reign, and multiply the Kingdom to release the King to your family, your city, your world.

God has not changed His plan. He has not changed His design. He has not changed His purposes for men and women. Every man on the planet needs you to take your place.

It begins when you say yes.

INTRODUCTION

"Men are from Earth; women are from Earth. Deal with it."
|| George Carlin[1]

If you have been in any sort of relationship with the opposite sex, you are well aware that men and women are different. We think differently. We relate differently. We view the world differently. Many of us have resigned ourselves to a lifetime of tolerating those differences and to a quiet (or a not-so-quiet) disconnect with the opposite sex. However, we are still the same, designed as two parts of the same whole. We carry the same purpose: to live as one flesh and rule and reign over planet Earth.

Women and men seem to be far from fulfilling the purpose of living in unity as one flesh. Instead, there is struggle and conflict between the sexes, confusion about who we are and who we are to each other. Many are confused about their roles, their genders, and their places in the world. Women continue to chase after men, looking for love. Men continue to oppress or abandon women instead of leading them and protecting them. Our marriages and our families are hurting. Divorce has ripped through many homes and hearts. Fractured men and women and their fractured relationships have created a fractured world.

It is time for that to end. The restoration and reconciliation of men and women is the answer.

We were designed as one flesh, made to function in perfect unity as a complement to each other. As George Carlin said, we are both from Earth; though he meant that in jest, the truth is we were made from the same dust, and any differences we have are meant to complement one another, to make us better together.

However, that is not what we have been taught. We have been taught that God made Adam, a man, in His image and that He gave Adam the big job of ruling the Earth. Then, we were told that Adam was lonely, so God made Eve, a woman, to be Adam's subordinate, to help him do his job. We married women were told that God wanted us to quietly submit to our husbands; as the helpers, we were supposed to "help," whatever that meant. Submission to your husband was taught from this paradigm: man is in charge and was made in God's image, and you are to be his helper. He leads and you follow. He decides and you submit. In this dynamic, there is no unity or peace. We were taught that when mankind fell, they brought upon themselves a curse, which was basically a fight for leadership and control. This is not accurate either. Unfortunately, for years and years, much of the Christian church culture and doctrine about men and women has been based on these incorrect concepts. These "concepts" have been repeated and handed down to each generation without question. We started with faulty interpretations, expanded on them, and built error on top of error. These misunderstandings are part of what has created struggle and conflict between us. These incorrect concepts of how and why God made us frame our understanding of who we are as women, diminish our voice, and interfere with how we relate to men. God wants to expose these incorrect concepts and how they affect women, and restore us to our place of power. To be restored as women, we must begin by correcting the errors.

We must go back to the beginning, which is where the Lord took me. Line by line and word by word, He revealed His original design and an even bigger picture emerged. There is a principle we can use to study the Bible called "The Law of First Mention." It states that to understand a subject, you begin by examining the first time the subject is mentioned. The basic concepts and patterns revealed in the first mention of a subject are a measuring stick we can use to interpret a subject from its simplest to its most complex interpretations. In other words, we use the fundamental design as the basis for the interpretation and then develop the subject in its complexities. Applying this principle to something in the natural, we could say that the basic design components of an airplane never changed from the Wright brothers' original design to the complex planes of today. The *basic* design is still present and unchanged, even though it has been added to and expanded.

Applying this law to the study of how God made men and women, we must examine the first mention of mankind. We will examine the creation, uncover the simplest concepts, and establish truths. After we establish the fundamental truths about men and women, we can then interpret more complex concepts, like the concept of submission, within the framework of the basic design. In the next chapters we are going to look into the creation story. We will challenge errors, and we will establish truths about how we were originally made, what really happened to us during the fall of mankind, and how we can get back to the perfect, original design.

The Lord started me on this journey of discovery with this scripture: "Behold, I will do a new thing, a woman will encompass a man" (Jeremiah 31:22). I pondered that scripture. I looked at it in several versions of the Bible and in the original Hebrew. I asked questions. I searched commentaries. I meditated on that scripture over and over, asking the Lord what it meant. After looking at many commentaries, I realized there is no clear consensus on what this scripture means. Then God began to reveal some key concepts to me. He had me look at every word in the original Hebrew and study its usage and meaning. Then He showed me that this was a picture of the original design for women. He began to reveal to me how and why He made us the way He did. He showed me that in the Jeremiah scripture, the word "new" actually means "renewed" or "restored." He is doing a renewed thing. He showed me that He is taking us back to the original design, which has been hidden for many years because of demonic influence, the power of culture, and the accepted yet erroneous teachings of the church. He wants to restore us to the original design in which two become one in His image. As I continued studying and praying, many other scriptures came together, and the picture became more and more clear. The original design, of a woman encircling and encompassing a man, was being restored.

As He brought further understanding, many other scriptures began to fall into place. Scriptures that I had pondered for years began to connect and I began to hear His heart for women. Women were not made as "helpers" in the sense that we have understood it; women were made as equals to men, equal in position and power and significance. We are equal but different, and we were not designed to *compete* but to *complete*. Our original design and functions are not what we have been taught; they are far

INTRODUCTION

more powerful. We were designed to encompass men with His Spirit. We were designed to be powerful influencers of men.

One day God put it on my heart that now is the time for the fulfillment of Jeremiah 31:22. Now is the time for God to restore women to the position that He originally intended them to hold. As He restores women, these restored women will also bring their influence and the Spirit of God to release the men. He created both male and female in His image, and they were to function as one, in power, unity, and agreement. The enemy knows the powerful, true position women have. He knows they have the power to encompass men, to guard their hearts, and to draw them into their right place. The enemy does anything he can to stop that, because when men and women live in their right positions, they reflect the image of God.

God began to show me how our design works against us, just as He explained to the first man and woman all the way back in the Garden of Eden. When Adam and Eve fell, their powerful, beautiful, original design gave way to a corrupted relationship between two orphans with broken hearts, conflicts, and struggle. Instead of encompassing Adam's heart with the Spirit of God, Eve would chase him, crave him, and turn to him to solve her inner ache for wholeness. This new relationship pattern would include a new response from man. He would now respond with pushing her down, pushing her away, or running away himself. Their unity was shattered, their relationship was compromised, and the original design was lost. *This is where we have lived for generations.*

To heal this, the Lord first wants to empower His beautiful, precious women. Through them He wants to reconcile the male/

female relationship and bring restoration to the men. When men and women live and function from their rightful positions, we reflect the image of God. We become Him on Earth in a way that we cannot do without each other. All women, married or single, can be restored to their original design and relate with men more in line with God's plan. Married or single, men and women can be restored to their original positions, which complement and complete each other. Women can be freed from their "need" for a man and instead function as his valuable and vital counterpart. She can receive all that he supplies to her, as well. Marriages will take a greater step towards the power they contain. His original concept for marriage was a relationship that reflected His image. He is a Trinity, a three-part being that is in perfect unity and agreement, powerful, creative. We were made in that image and as a two-part/one-flesh leadership team, we were given complete authority to take dominion over the planet. How many couples do you see who are in unity and agreement? How many marriages do you see today that actually take dominion over the world's problems? Most couples can barely take dominion over their own families or even their own individual selves! It is time for that to change.

Second, God wants to release the fathers on this planet to set the stage for His return. When men are restored, they take their place as fathers and leaders. When fathers are engaged and when their hearts are turned to their children, then we will truly see cultural change. Fatherhood leadership can change the world. Imagine the majority of men full of God—protecting and not abusing, leading and not exploiting, empowering and not oppressing the women and children of the world. When men and women are restored, change will come. This will open wide the doors and truly prepare the way for the Lord.

INTRODUCTION

The Lord is calling to His people:

"The eye of the Lord is upon His people. It is time to reclaim what so many of you have cried for and desired. You may not have understood what you lost or the full ramifications of what happened at the fall of mankind. You may not fully understand what I have planned and am about to do. However, you do not need to understand; you only need to obey. I am ready to release my women to return to their original design and purpose. I am about to restore all that they have lost. All women, single or married, were created to carry my heart to mankind and they are going to be freed to release My Spirit in greater measures. I am about to restore the holiness and sanctity of marriage; marriages will begin to recover the power that they contain. All that is hidden will be revealed. There is more revelation for Me to release. Ask Me for it and seek it. Come and experience the revelation of My original design and purposes. Ask Me for more, and I will gladly pour it out upon you. I will cause you to walk in complete oneness in your marriages. I will cause you to flow in the unity and blessings and power of the Kingdom. See that you walk inside the Kingdom, and the Kingdom will overtake you and cause you to recapture all that was lost.

Jesus has come and did come and continues to come to seek and save that which my children lost. All that was lost—the positions, the power, the unity, the value of My women, the holiness and power of marriage, the union of male and female—will be restored and will release more of Me on the planet. You will experience more of My Spirit and more of My power. I am bringing greater dimensions of Myself to Earth, and one of the ways that I will do this is through My restored women and then through your marriages."

The Lord is aware of how He made us and who He made us. He is aware of the power we hold as women, and He knows that we can influence the hearts of men. Now is the time. Change is coming.

1

WE WERE CREATED TO ENCOMPASS

"But at the beginning of creation God made them male and female."
∥ MARK 10:6 (NIV)

"Male and female he created them; and blessed them, and called their name Adam, in the day when they were created."
∥ GENESIS 5:2 (KJV)

"Eve was not taken out of Adam's head to top him, neither out of his feet to be trampled on by him, but out of his side to be equal with him, under his arm to be protected by him, and near his heart to be loved by him."
∥ MATTHEW HENRY[2]

In order to fully participate in what God wants to do for women, we must understand how we were designed and who we really are. This is the foundation we will build in the first few chapters. There is much to unpack as we apply truth to past teachings and old mindsets. After we build our foundation, the latter chapters will offer practical application and further understanding.

Let's start at the beginning, in the first chapters of Genesis:

> *"And God said 'Let Us [Father, Son, and Holy Spirit] make mankind in Our image, after Our likeness [not physical, but a spiritual personality and moral likeness]; and let them*

> *have complete authority over the fish of the sea, the birds of the air, the cattle, and over the entire Earth, and over everything that creeps and crawls on the Earth. So God created man in His own image, in the image and likeness of God He created him; male and female he created them. And God blessed them [granting them certain authority] and said to them, 'Be fruitful, multiply, and fill the Earth, and subjugate it [putting it under your power]; and rule over (dominate) the fish of the sea, the birds of the air, and every living thing that moves upon the Earth.'"*
> —Genesis 1:26–28, AMP

Much of what we have heard in the church about the creation of mankind begins with the assumption that when God made mankind in His image, the word "mankind" actually meant a "male." This concept that God created one single male in His image and that He named this male "Adam" is inaccurate. This one small misinterpretation leads to large errors when we look at men and women and the relationship between them. We will begin by correcting this thinking. God did *not* make a male and named that man Adam; that is not the story of the creation of mankind. If we look more closely at the text of Genesis 1:26: "Let Us make mankind in Our image..." tells a different story. It does not say "man" or "male"; in the Hebrew language the gendered word for "man" or "male" is *"iysh"*[3] and that word is not used here. (The word *iysh* appears much later in the story.) In the Genesis 1:26–28 text, the word "man" is the word *"adam,"*[3] which most accurately translates as "mankind" (H120). The word *adam* comes from the root word *"adamah,"*[3] which translates as "Earth." Taking this concept back to the text, we see that when God set out to make man in His image, He meant that He would make *adam*, meaning mankind. What God really said was "Let us make *Mankind* in our image"—and not an individual male.

Our first truth is that *mankind* is created in His image, and what, exactly, *is* the image of God? His image is a Trinity. The Trinity is a three-part being, and each part has its own distinct function and personality. The Trinity functions in perfect order and unity. John 5:18–19 shows a glimpse of what this unity looks like. In this passage, Jesus first says He is equal with the Father and yet He *does only* what the *Father* does and does not act on His own. In John 12:49, Jesus says He can *only speak* what the *Father* is speaking. We see agreement and unity in the Trinity. In John 15:26, we see that the Holy Spirit will come and testify of Jesus; there is agreement again. First Corinthians 2:10–16 shows us that the very heart of the Father God is *only known* by the Holy Spirit, who searches it. Last, 1 John 5:7-8 in the Amplified version says, "For there are *three* witnesses: the Spirit and the water and the blood; and these three *are in agreement* [their testimony is perfectly consistent]." There are three separate parts of one God, yet all three are in agreement, which is unity. Jesus prayed for all His future followers in John 17:21, "That all of them may be one, Father, *just as you are in me and I am in you*. May they also be in us so that the world may believe that you have sent me" (NIV, emphasis added). The Trinity was present at creation, and it is speaking as One, in unity. The threefold God communicated their desires in what they would create, and they decided to create mankind in their likeness and image. When God said, "Let Us make mankind in Our image," part of the image He was referring to is the image of the Trinity. Therefore, we can say that mankind was patterned after the Trinity, a multi-faceted being that communicates, decides and functions in complete unity. This is also apparent in Genesis 5:2, where it says that He called *their* name adam, or He called their name "*mankind*." The word "their" implies that mankind was made with more than one part, yet mankind was also a unified being like the Trinity.

This is the likeness we were created after, the likeness of God. Mankind was originally designed as a multifaceted being that functions in unity and order, with released power and creativity, and in the same likeness and image of our powerful Creator. We will look at this concept many more times in this book; for now, let's answer this question: in what way was mankind *multifaceted*? The Trinity is made up of the Father, the Son, and the Holy Spirit, but what are the parts of the original creation called mankind?

Genesis 1:27 says, "So God created man in *His own image*, in the image of God He created them; *male and female* he created *them*..." (NIV, emphasis added).

This passage shows that just as the Trinity includes more than one separate but distinct personality, mankind was also created with more than one separate but distinct personality: male and female. In the original design, male and female were combined in one being, to function as the Trinity in agreement and unity, in a dynamic flow of energy and power. God's desire for mankind was to be as He is, a united yet multifaceted being. God is not referring to Himself as just a "male" and He is not expressed through just one gender. Since God is not confined to defining Himself as only one gender, in the same way, mankind, as made in the likeness of God, *cannot* be solely male, but we can say that mankind was also more than one gender.

There are multiple places in the scriptures that give us a picture of God as a male. He's referred to as our Father and our Husband and our Bridegroom. The Lord uses masculine terms to refer to Himself in multiple places in the scriptures, and we commonly use male pronouns when we refer to God. He chose to take the form of a man when He came to Earth in a human body, as the man Jesus. Primarily the Lord is referred to as a male and in masculine terms. However, several places in the Word also describe God in a way that makes Him sound like He also expresses Himself as a female. In Genesis 17:1, God introduces Himself to Abram as "El Shaddai." This term translates as "Destroyer" but also as "Breasty One," or "The Mighty Breasty One," which is a feminine and even motherly description.[4] In Hosea 11:3-4, the Lord describes Himself as a Mother, teaching His children to walk, cradling them in His arms, bending down to feed them. In Hosea 13:8, He says He is like a mother bear robbed of her cubs. In Deuteronomy 32:11-12, He says He is like a mother eagle, teaching us to fly. In Isaiah 66:13, He says, "As a mother comforts her child, so will I comfort you" (NIV). In Isaiah 49:15, He compares Himself to a nursing mother, and in Isaiah 42:14, He compares Himself to a woman in labor, birthing her children. Jesus says in both Matthew 23:37 and Luke 13:34 that He is like a mother hen, longing to gather her children. There are many other references to God as both a Father and a Mother. He is Spirit, that is clear in John 4:24, and Spirit is not limited to human terms or definitions. Though we are made in His image, we only reflect *part* of that image; He is certainly *more* than His image. He transcends our human understanding and terms. In this, I think it is suitable to say that God is genderless. He is Spirit. He is neither solely male nor solely female; He can express Himself as either gender or both. For mankind, we can say this: we represent the image of God, who cannot be explained with human definitions or confine Himself to one gender. There is something in both male and female that God expresses Himself through. This is the truth of who we are. We start with our first building block of truth: God created mankind (*adam*) after His image, as an expression of both male and female in one being, a being that functions in complete unity.

When your understanding of creation begins with the misinterpretation that God created a man, as a single male, then you are saying that only men were made in God's image. This interpretation creates more questions and provides fewer answers. How is the design of a male like God? Since God is a multifaceted Trinity, are males designed also as multifaceted? Since God also expresses Himself as female, how is a male also a female? In Genesis it says, "male and female He created them" (NIV), and if we accept that God made a male in His image, then where was the female? If we erroneously believe that men were the only ones who were made in the likeness of God, then only men would have power and authority. Only men are called to rule and reign and multiply? This misinterpretation of our design allows men and women very little unity and no equality. When we base our understanding on the misinterpretation that God made a male in His image, it limits our identity as women, and we are crippled in how we relate to men.

When we begin with the truth that mankind, both male and female, were created in God's image as a multifaceted being that was designed to function in unity like the Trinity, we have shared power, and there are no limits on either gender. This is the truth of our original design: men and women are interdependent and equal in power, authority, and purpose. There was no distinction in God's eyes—just one being that He called "Adam." Any other insight about men and women will rest on these two foundational concepts: (1) mankind is a multifaceted being that functions similarly to the Trinity; and (2) mankind is simultaneously both genders, male and female. These two truths lay the important foundation that women and men have equal power, authority, and responsibility to rule, and we were designed to function together as two separate and distinct identities, yet one being.

In his book *Unlocking the Torah Text; Bereishit*,[5] Shmuel Goldin says, "One authority in the Talmud maintains that God originally created man *d'yo partzuf panim*, 'with two faces.' Imbedded within Adam were both a male and female human being. As is often the case, the rabbis are conveying a profound idea in the form of what seems to be a simple tale."[6] There are other writings in rabbinical literature on this subject that suggest that not only did mankind have "two faces," but that these two faces of the first created human being faced in opposite directions. Mankind was one being with two "faces," or more easily explained, two "souls."[7]

Looking more closely at the creation story, we see that each "face" or "soul" existed while they were together in one flesh. In Genesis 2:7, we are told that the Lord formed mankind from the dust of the ground and breathed the breath of life into mankind, and mankind became a living soul. If you dig through that passage in the Hebrew, it actually says that He breathed the breath of lives. Plural.[8] The word for life is *"chaya"* and in this passage it is in the plural form *"chayim"* or "lives."[9] I believe that "breath of lives" was written in the plural because when He breathed into mankind, He was actually breathing into *two separate beings* that were combined into one; He breathed into both of them and it is the very breath of God that made them, mankind, a "living soul" (Genesis 2:7). Why else would "breath of lives" have been pluralized? What other life was being breathed into? It is because mankind contained more than one soul. There are other clues that support this concept. With a closer look into the story, we see that when female is taken out of male and given her own physical body, there is evidence that she was already a living soul while inside him. When the female is pulled out of the male and is physically completed, God doesn't breathe into her to make her a living soul. God doesn't build her a body of her own and then need to put *life* or a soul into her. Why? God does not breathe the breath of life into her *then* because He *already* had, when she was inside the male. She *already* was a living soul. She became a living soul when she was inside the male, and God breathed into *them* the breath of *lives*. When He breathed into mankind, they *separately and together* became living souls, made in the image of God. Even the fact that in Genesis 5 God refers to "them" as "male and female" infers that she had her *own* personality or distinct personhood separate from him.

Male and female received life and became souls, living beings, at the same time inside one flesh. Inside the male, female had an essence, a soul. In Hebrew, the word used for "soul" is *nephesh*, and it means living being, person, desires, life, emotion, appetite, heart, will.[10] In *Merriam-Webster's Dictionary*, it says a soul[11] is a person's total self, the moral and emotional nature of a human being, the immaterial essence of a person. You could combine these definitions to say that a soul is the immaterial part of your being: your mind, your will, and your emotions. It is your essence and what is "you" on the inside. So when God breathed into them the breath of lives, He made two separate *souls* within one body. Female was present; she had a soul and was a living being inside the male, who also had a soul. Since she was a living soul, she had feelings, she had thoughts, she had a will, she had her own desires, and she was her own person, a living soul, inside of male. As a living being, she could think and feel and desire and have the full functioning of a person, yet her body was actually *his* body. This is how we were originally designed.

We also know she was inside of him because when God eventually separates them, He removes her from the male. Even in the New Testament, 1 Corinthians 11:7–8 does not say that man was taken from woman but that "woman was taken from man" (NIV). The idea of something being "taken" out of something else implies that it exists already. Something must be in existence to be taken from something else! In Genesis 2:22, the Lord removes the man's rib: "from the rib He had taken from the man, the Lord God made a woman" (KJV). The word "made" in this text is the Hebrew word *banah*[12] (H1129), which means to build, rebuild, cause to continue. In the rest of the creation story there are two words that are primarily used to describe creation, the two words that mean "created" or "fashioned" or "made." It is during the creation of the physical body of female that we see the word *banah*; female is *continued from* what God had already made of female when He created mankind in one being. He took what was female's substance, her cells, her essence, her soul, and continued to build her into a separate physical being. He used a specific word that differed from most of the creation story because she was not a "brand new creation." This word *banah* is also seen in the Old Testament in the context of building a temple or a city or an altar. Altars, buildings, and cities are built from other created things like wood and rock. We can paraphrase Genesis 2:22 and say that the Lord God took what was her substance, which was contained within the male, and with the cells of her soul, He took from what He had *already* created and continued to make her into a fully separate physical being.

There are other clues that suggest that she was a living soul inside him. For instance, even the male was aware and understood this concept. After the Lord pulls her out of him and makes her, continues her, into her own physical being, He doesn't say anything to the male. He doesn't say, "I took her from you," nor does the Father give an explanation of how or where they were connected. Yet the man takes one look at her and is able to recognize that she was taken from him. Without any explanation from the Lord, he looks at her and says, "bone of my bone, flesh of my flesh" (Genesis 2:23, KJV). He understands and knows that she was inside of him, a part of his being. Perhaps in some way he may have felt the difference internally. He no longer held her inside of himself. Could she also understand her experience of being inside him? It appears so, because she was a living soul inside him when they were one being. A living soul that had thoughts, feelings, desires. As a living soul, she must have experienced their connection because she *was* alive in him!

Adam also knew she had been taken out of him because I believe that his internal dialogue changed. He knew that the living soul that used to communicate with him in some internal way was now outside of his body; their internal communication had ceased. She had been inside of him as a living soul with thoughts and feelings and ideas, and she had communicated with him as a living soul inside of his body. It is not clear how they communicated; this is something that is hard for our minds to grasp. We do know, however, that they *did* communicate. We can accept this truth with confidence because they were designed in the likeness of the Trinity, who also communicates one to another. There are many places in the Bible that show us the communication of the Trinity. For example, they are clearly communicating at the creation of mankind when they say, "Let Us make man in Our image." In the same way as the Trinity communicates while in one being, male and female could communicate in the likeness of the Trinity. It is hard for us to grasp this, but it was easy for them as they lived it. They lived as one being; they knew what it was like. We will look at this in more detail in a later chapter, but for now we will just say that they could communicate—she, from in a very deep internal place inside him, in and near his ribs, which surrounded his heart.

How else might he have known that she was taken from him? How did he know what had happened? We can assume that he felt the pain or the sensitivity of his side. Every single movement of your body is supported in some way or affected in some way by your ribs. To twist, turn, lift, or bend, you need your ribs for support. I think Adam felt the pain and understood, "Oh, here is where she lived, she is bone of my bone and flesh of my flesh. The living soul that used to be inside of me is now standing in front of me; she is from my bones and my flesh." He could have pointed to the place where his rib was removed and explained to her: "*Here* is where you lived." He knew that she was inside of him and now he knew where, exactly, she lived. She in turn, could say, "I was at your side, near your heart, tucked under your arms." She very likely felt the vulnerability of no longer being safely inside, under his arm. They could understand that she was inside of him and he contained her; they understood that because they *lived* it. They lived as one flesh.

She surrounded or encompassed him, and he literally contained her. The word "contain" suggests that something is designed so that something else can be placed within it. Merriam-Webster's Dictionary defines the word "contain"[13] as "to hold, to have, to have something inside another thing." This is the original design of mankind, that male contained female. Where did he contain her? Woman was taken from the man's side. Her actual physical position inside of the man was under or inside one or more of his ribs. In the Genesis 2:22 text, the Hebrew word is *tsela* and it translates to "rib" or "side"[14]. This is where her soul originally dwelled. This is where he contained her, at his side, in or under his rib, under the protection of his arms. She dwelt within the ribcage, which encompassed and surrounded him. Not only does the rib cage support all the body's movements, it surrounds and protects important organs—most importantly the heart and lungs. The rib cage also surrounds the area of the body where our spirit and soul dwells. This is where she originally lived. Her substance literally encompassed his physical, spiritual, and emotional being, and he contained her there, at his side, under his arm, near the deepest, most intimate parts of him.

For many years, the Lord had directed me to the scripture passage Jeremiah 31:22: "Behold I will do a new thing, woman will encompass a man" (NIV). I especially pondered the word "encompass" and meditated on it. "Encompass," as defined in *Merriam-Webster's Dictionary*, means to surround, circle, encircle. In Hebrew it is *cabab*[15] (H5437), which means surround, circle, make a circuit, flow around, turn around, turn back. We will return to this scripture and this concept many more times in this book. For now, I want to establish that this is the most basic, foundational part of our original design. God revealed to me that this is the key to how He created mankind: a male contained a female, as they were two living souls in one flesh. She was created from the very same *adamah* (Earth) at the very same time that he was created. She received the very same breath of life, and they became living souls together in one body. The truth of our original design is that *man contained woman, and woman encompassed man.* God's design for us has not changed, and from this design we see the relationship dynamic at work. It is the same design and dynamic that He has for us today. As women are to restored their position as "encompassers," men will respond as the "containers." This position as "encompasser" is rich in meaning, and we will examine it more closely in the next chapter. In the chapters to come, we will look at these concepts in more practical detail and will apply them to our everyday lives. However, I do not want to move too quickly past the incredible truth of our original design and what it means for men and women. Together with men, we were made in God's image. We carry God's heart for mankind. Women were made to be powerful influencers of men. We are valuable, and men need us; mankind needs us! Together, men and women carry the power and presence of God.

In the original design, when man and woman were as one flesh, they experienced the power, blessings, and presence of God. His love and presence and the stamp of His likeness were upon them. In Genesis 1:28, we see that as soon as the Lord created mankind, He blessed them. Isn't that amazing? They hadn't done a single thing, yet they received grace from God and were immediately blessed. They began life by receiving from God the breath of lives, and then, as one flesh, mankind was blessed. Like the Trinity, mankind was in unity with each other and with the Lord; the original couple had unbroken fellowship with the Creator. In this perfect state of unity and togetherness, mankind was blessed and then was given the amazing task to rule. Genesis 1:28 says, "God blessed them and said to them, 'Be fruitful and increase in number; fill the Earth and subdue it. Rule over the fish in the sea and the birds in the sky and over every living creature that moves on the ground'" (NIV). Mankind, in the likeness of the Trinity and in the delegated power of the Father, is as God's very ruling presence on Earth. In unity and blessed favor, mankind lived in harmony, he contained her and she encompassed him.

If we compare this picture with the Christian church's interpretation of mankind, that has been taught for years, there are vast differences in how men and women are represented. If we accept the church's longstanding, inaccurate mindset, then we are diminished and limited. This inaccurate belief does not make room for the Trinity or the power of God to be expressed through men and women. It not only limits individual men and women; it also limits them as a *couple*. It limits the power of God that can be experienced in marriage, and the responsibility to release Him through our marriages is nonexistent. This picture of creation is not only erroneous, but also it is sad.

What we have understood about men and women and their relationship is far from the real picture. Women are not acknowledged as joint and equal with men in our call nor in our power. Women are not seen as being made in God's image. Women are seen as second, as an afterthought that was created only *for* men, not *from* or *with* them. This belief creates a loss for men, too, as they are left unaware of how vital women are to them; it keeps men from their full potential and keeps them from functioning in their full power.

The truth is that we were designed to function *together*. Men and women are equal in position, in power, and in purpose. We are best together. We need each other. We were and are blessed together, in unity. Man and woman were present from the beginning as two living souls who ruled and reigned over planet Earth; they were separate and distinct individuals and yet combined, made in the image of God. That is our true identity. With each concept about men and women that we expose, challenge, and reframe with truth, our identities are improved and expanded, and we are empowered.

WAS ADAM LONELY?

There are still more errors we have believed that need to be exposed! The misinterpretation of not only *how* we were created but *why* women were created is also extremely harmful to our identity. We are going to challenge that thinking and establish another building block of truth about the purpose for the creation of woman. If you've been in the Christian church for any amount of time, you will have heard at least one person say that Adam was lonely and this is why God created Eve. It is taught that God had Adam name the animals so that he could see how lonely he was. That could not be more wrong. We were not made because Adam was lonely. Adam was not given the task of naming the animals as an object lesson to show him how lonely he was and how deeply he needed a partner. I don't believe that at all.

First of all, it isn't logical to say that he was lonely. We know and have already seen that he contained the female. They were two in one being. How could they be lonely? They were not alone, and he did not *need* a partner; he already *had* one, she was inside him! Not only was she inside him, but they functioned in peaceful unity together and with the Father. Since he wasn't lonely or alone, he didn't need a woman to make him less lonely. If women came into the Earth so men wouldn't be lonely, then wouldn't it say that in other places in the scriptures? Why doesn't the Bible tell women to be on the lookout for loneliness in men? Wouldn't there be a verse including some direction from the Lord saying, "Woman, make sure your man is not lonely," or, "Women, it's your job to keep your husbands relationally satisfied"? It doesn't say that anywhere in the Bible, because that's not why we were created. That isn't our job. Women were not created because a man was lonely. Naming the animals was not meant to make man feel or acknowledge his loneliness. However, it is true that the task of naming the animals was an object lesson for them; it just wasn't about loneliness.

Right before they begin naming the animals, the Lord says, "Mankind, it is not good for you to be *alone*" (Genesis 2:18, NIV, emphasis added). This is where the idea of "loneliness" comes from; the word "alone" has been misinterpreted to mean "lonely." However, when you look at this text in the Hebrew, the word "alone" is "*bad*"[16] (H905); it actually means "sole" or "parts of" or "of itself."[17]

What the Lord really says is that it is not good for mankind, as two living souls in one flesh, to be "sole" or "of itself," meaning "in one body." It was not the best thing for them to be *sole*. That is a much different message than male being lonely and woman filling that need. The truth is that it was no longer best for His creation to remain in one flesh. They were created together for a reason, and they were separated into two bodies for a reason and the Lord was preparing them for the lesson that would explain this. Keep in mind that when the Lord said, "It is not good for my new creation of Mankind to be alone, of itself, and sole," He said that to *them*. Mankind, both male and female, heard the Lord say that it wasn't good for them to be in one body or "sole," and this statement was their preparation before their task. That seed of thought began to germinate and grow as they performed the task that they were given together.

From that thought, that it wasn't good for them to be sole, they set out to name every created thing. As each animal species came before mankind to be named, they could see that each animal was created with two separate bodies—one male, one female. The animals, birds, and living things were created in two separate beings; this was the first of their lessons. It became obvious to them that they were made as one, not as two. Genesis 2:20

says that in all of this, mankind did not find their counterpart. The lesson they needed to learn was not that man *needed* a partner, because he *had* one, but they needed to understand that functioning in one body wasn't the best way to *have* a partner or counterpart. This is what they had been prepared to learn; as they named the animals, seeing them in pairs, partners in separate bodies, they could see what two bodies of male and female are able to do.

Naming every animal and living thing was no small task, and it probably took some time to accomplish it. I imagine lots of animals were waiting around for their turn to be named. They were likely grazing, napping, and quite likely mating. By the time some of the animal couples were presented before mankind to be named, they could have already reproduced and had an offspring. Mankind saw not only what it looks like to have a male and female of each species, but also they see how the two, male and female, mated and multiplied. This is the ultimate object lesson in the "birds and the bees" from a loving Father to His special creation. Now, they could understand their own responsibility to fill the planet, to multiply, which was their call from the beginning. It could make sense now, as they had seen animals, males and females of each species, in separate bodies, multiply and reproduce. Malachi 2:15 says, "Has not the one God made you? You belong to him in body and spirit. And what does the one God seek? Godly offspring" (NIV). Certainly, after their task of naming the animals, mankind learned the lessons. They now could understand what male/female counterparts were and how they themselves were two souls in one body. They could understand that if they were in separate bodies, they could join their bodies to reproduce and multiply. They could understand *why* it wasn't good for them to be "sole." God had prepared them to learn this. This is often God's way of teaching—to lead us into learning, and here we see Him leading mankind into some profound lessons.

Again, the Lord had His perfect timing in this. He told them that it was not good to be in one body, and as soon as they were shown the purpose for separate male and female bodies, it was time to actually separate them. They were ready for their next step of maturity—to become two separate bodies that could still function as one, as they had been. As God does with all His children, when they were ready, He led them to the next step. God could have created them in two separate bodies from the beginning, but then they would not have been designed after His likeness and image. The design needed to be both male and female in one being; they needed to know how to function as one being, like the Trinity. They were designed to be one flesh, in the image of God; they knew how to function as one, and would return to that place of physical oneness as they saw the animals do. They could also continue to function as one flesh both spiritually and emotionally, *as they had been* since they were created. They understood their functions in their design, they had experienced how to live as one. They could understand that mankind, men and women, were designed to function as one flesh. We need to know that today too. We need to know that that is our original design. Plus, we need to know *how* to function as one, just as they had. Genesis *commands* us that we *are* to live as one flesh when we marry (2:24), and they are our example, the two-part/one-flesh team, as they lived from the beginning.

INTRODUCING THE "EZER KENNEGDO"

There is another misinterpretation that is vital for us to expose and challenge. We must return to the Genesis passage and consider Genesis 2:18–25. After, the Lord said it is not good for mankind to be "of itself," He then said that He would make (continue creating) the female, as it was time for mankind to be separated. He said that He would *banah* (continue) to make "a helper," which is translated as *ezer kennegdo*[18] in the Hebrew. The common misinterpretation of this is that woman was to be the "helpmate," but the connotation of this term is far from an accurate translation. *Ezer*[19] (H5828) has the meaning "help or aid," but it comes from the root word *azar*, which means to protect or to succor (often in a military sense). It is a term used in connection with the Holy Spirit; He is called our *ezer* or *azar*, this word includes the concept of someone bringing God's strength to a situation. We can understand the Holy Spirit as our *ezer*, coming to fight for us and alongside us and bringing His strength to our situations. This word *ezer* is so much bigger than saying "helper." Could we really, with good conscience, say the Holy Spirit is just our "helper/assistant"? That is a diminished and inaccurate picture of who He is! Here He is in Psalm 54:4: "Behold, God is my *helper*; the Lord is the upholder of my life" (KJV, emphasis added). In Psalm 70:5: "Make haste to me, O God! You are my *help* and my deliverer" (KJV, emphasis added). In Psalm 124:8: "Our *help* is in the name of the LORD, Who made heaven and Earth" (KJV, emphasis added). The Creator of the Universe delivers us from our enemies, fights our battles for us in both the seen and unseen realms, upholds and sustains us, and could we say that He is our "assistant"? It would be better to say that the Holy Spirit is one who comes alongside us and empowers us and helps us to fight. At times He even fights for us. There is nowhere that implies an inferior or subordinate position; on the contrary, *ezer* is a position of strength.

Joining with *ezer* is the Hebrew word *kennegdo*[20] (H5048), which is commonly translated as "suitable for" but it can mean counterpart or "counter-mate," and this is where the idea of a "helpmate" came from. This error in translation was made as the *King James Bible* was written. This word "helpmeet"[21] was a common word in English culture of the day. It eventually was the word used for women as the "helper," but the actual Hebrew words mean so much more. The word *kennegdo* has a much greater meaning than counter-mate. It also means "holds strength" or even "opposing strength or strength against," and it infers a counterbalance to strength. An *ezer kennegdo* could fight against you. We will talk about this more when we look at the Fall, as we see that females can be an equal strength against males. For now, however, we will look at this concept according to God's original perfect design and will consider how the female is the the one who helps with opposite strength, the opposite strength counterpart, or the one who fights with a complement of strength to the male. The Bible does not say that we were made as "helpers" in the sense that we are only assistants to man's important purpose. That is not the word of God. What it does say is that we were made as man's *ezer kennegdo*; we were made to fight alongside man, to bring him our strength, to be a strong, equal counterpart, to be an opposite strength and a complement. Women are one half of the whole of mankind, with the same joint responsibility to be fruitful, to multiply, to subdue the planet, to rule and reign over planet Earth. Woman was given the same purpose as man, when she was inside him. We are dependent upon him as he is also dependent upon us; again, this is the picture of the Trinity. Each part of the Trinity is an equal counterpart to the other; each is equal in strength. Each has its own personality. Each has its own identity, in a sense, yet both work together in unity.

To paraphrase this Genesis scripture, it says: "It is not good for mankind to be sole, in one body. It is time to continue making the female into her own body, the equal power counterpoint to the male. They will continue to fight alongside each other; she will bring to him her strength, as they together rule, reign, and take dominion. This is who she was inside of him: surrounding him at his rib cage, supporting every movement, influencing him, and fulfilling the same purposes—yet as a separate living soul inside of him. She was already his *ezer kennegdo*. They could understand the concept of *ezer kennegdo* because they lived it as one flesh. They understood all they heard from the Father and all they saw in their task to name the animals. Now they are ready. It was time to separate them into two beings, male and female. They are put to sleep, and she is taken from him, and God continues to make her and them into two separate beings. When he awakens, he knows and understands. He awakens and knows something has happened—most likely because he feels the pain and loss at his side and the internal change from the loss of her soul in him. With the amazing revelation they have just received, they now understand that even though the one has become two, the two are still one and must remain as one. They have seen the animals and know that physically, there is a way to join their bodies, and they can still physically be 'one flesh.' They already experienced being one flesh in their soul, and they know how they function together as one in the spirit and soul realm."

As soon as the Lord finishes making the female, He presents her to the male. Genesis 2:23 says, "The man said, 'This at last is bone of my bones and flesh of my flesh; she shall be called Woman for she was taken out of Man'" (ESV). It is interesting to note that the word used for "man" here is *iysh*,[22] which means "of a male gender" in Hebrew. It is the first time the word for gender is used in the entire creation story. Man says "she shall be called Woman," using the word *ishshah*, which means "woman/wife" or "female." The first time we see the differentiation of gender in the Bible is when we actually have a gender appear in mankind. This is an important truth. The words for "man" and "woman" as separate genders now appear in the scriptures as man is able to distinguish that he is man and she is woman. Previously, the only word for man and woman was *adam*, which meant mankind. This is evidence for the revelation mankind had been given. They know they are now man and woman. They understand that they are the male and female. In one body they were one flesh without one gender, and now that they are in two bodies, they are male and female, or man and woman. It is not God but it is the man who calls her "Woman."

It is also interesting to note that anytime we see someone being named in the Bible, it is a significant moment and often marks a significant event. She now has her own separate physical body, and with this significant event, she receives a new name. Every name Woman is given paints a picture of who God made women to be. The first name she was given, *adam*, or "mankind," was given by God. He names her mankind because she is an equal part of mankind that carries the female expression of Him—the comfort, nurture, and love He gives to mankind. By naming us "mankind," He expresses that we carry an equal responsibility to release Him to the rest of mankind. We women carry the "mother" expression of God as well as His compassionate heart. We are the nurturers, the comforters, and the lovers. Second, the Lord calls Woman the "encompasser" and also the *ezer kennegdo*. Those names suggest that Woman is the perfect counterpart to Man; she is the equal-strength helper who surrounds his heart. She is his internal support and he needs her to bring her strength to him to take dominion, rule and reign with him. Women have a powerful place on Earth; we are part of God's image and hold a vital position within mankind. We are not less than, but equal in our calling. Our identity is clearly seen in the names He gave us, the names that define who we are. When Man names her Woman, he is saying, "You are a part of me. You came from my body. You are female, my wife. I need you as you need me; we are parts of each other." This is still who we are today.

What we are told next in the Genesis passage, immediately following the separation, is that "man will leave his father and his mother and cling to his wife, and they will become one flesh" (2:24, ISV). This verse was written by Moses when he wrote the book of Genesis. This was not said to Man and Woman when they were separated. It didn't need to be said at that time. First of all, they would not have had a reference point for this comment. God was their Father. They weren't leaving Him in order to marry; that would have not made sense. This concept was added for our understanding. It was added to the story so we know that we become one flesh when we marry. It is the immediate instruction following the text of the separation and completion of Woman. This instruction is placed here for us to know that this is the design: two as one. The design never changed. The original male and female understood the concept of one flesh through revelation and experience. They already knew how to function as one. At one time her living soul was actually inside his body and able to communicate with him. They knew that they were one flesh and were to remain as such, even in separate bodies. They experienced this and could explain it to their children and grandchildren. The immediate generations that followed could have had some sort of understanding as Adam and Eve explained to them. However, for us today, this concept is something we have not understood and the example has been far removed. Even so, the Lord had Moses (the author of the book of Genesis) add this verse for our benefit so we don't miss the crucial concept that all married men and women of every generation were designed to be one flesh—and commanded to live as such—even though we were born into separate male and female bodies. Nevertheless, the command of the Lord has remained, we are to function as one flesh, and today He is making sure we will know what that means. Just like Adam and Eve, we will understand, too. We are not just reclaiming what we have *lost* but what we have never *seen*.

These revelations are our foundation for practical application. God made mankind in His image. Mankind was designed as a multipart being with more than one gender. It is a being that is in unity of purpose and function and designed to stay in unity as one flesh. He created mankind as both male and female in one body and called them adam. He blessed them and told them that together they were to multiply, to fill the planet and to reign and rule over the planet, together, as an equal and opposite strength leadership team.

This is a profoundly different interpretation of the creation of mankind and the design of men and women than we have previously understood. It gives us an entirely different perspective of who we are as men and women and who we are together. Women are not just helpmates who assist men in their important call to rule and reign. Women are an essential part of mankind. We are powerful, valuable complements to men and are so much more than what we have previously been told. For the purpose of this book, we will focus primarily on the woman's position as "encompasser." In the next chapter we will look more carefully at what it means to be an encompasser and will begin understanding how to encompass. In the coming chapters, we will look further at the power of woman that has been stolen from us and from mankind.

THE NEW WOMEN'S MOVEMENT

For now, the Lord wants to say this to us, as women:

"I made mankind in My image. I am a multifaceted being that is so much more than just one of any gender. Mankind walks in My image and is able to create and multiply and reproduce and take authority over this planet as rulers. Men and women have a special bond, and when they join together, they have the ability to function in total unity and harmony, and I am there to bless and to release power and authority through them. My presence and power are released through their marriages when they function as one flesh. They show the world who I am. With Me and together, men and women are to rule in unity. This unity releases power. They were not created for a power struggle. They were made as two separate souls that can and will function as one, in order and agreement and power and unity. This is the time to recapture that original design. This is the time to restore what was stolen from My men and women. I am grieved by what was lost and the suffering that has followed. I want to act. I want to heal you and bless you and protect you, My precious daughters, from oppression and abuse. I want to protect your children. I want to release your men. I am here to show you this new way to relate and to reveal to you how to live as I created you to live. I am here to restore. I made man to be the container, the protector, the covering of women, and I made woman to be the encompasser, the influencer, the watchful eye over the heart of man. I have never changed My mind nor changed the design or purposes of mankind. Mankind was made to rule this planet in My authority, in the authority that I gave them when I created them. I am releasing this again in a new wave of anointing. I am breathing on you again. I am beginning this work with women, and you will soon understand why. Any woman who says yes to Me and allows me to heal and restore her can know that although this journey may be difficult, it will end with unity, peace, power, and the discovery and fulfillment of her purpose and the purposes of those around her. You simply must be willing in heart and mind, and I will do what is needed. I will show you the way, and I will give you the strength to finish. I am not a liar, and I will not disappoint. Let Me bring you back to your place as encompasser. I say to you, My women, My loves, My fair ones—come with Me. For the springtime has come."

2

ENCOMPASSER, THE ORIGINAL DESIGN OF WOMAN

"A woman shall encompass a man."
‖ JEREMIAH 31:22

"The especial genius of women I believe to be electrical in movement, intuitive in function, spiritual in tendency."
‖ MARGARET FULLER

"The woman's vision is deep, the man's far reaching. With the man the world is his heart, with the woman, the heart is her world."
‖ BETTY GRABLE

So far in our journey we have looked in some detail at the story of the creation of mankind. We have seen that God created mankind in His image, a Trinity, multifaceted and both male and female. We have seen the original design, two souls made in one body and then separated into two bodies. They are now Man and Woman, yet the Lord calls them both Adam or mankind. Regardless of whether they are in one body or two, God does not change their function or the dynamics of their relationship. Even though they are separate bodies, they are to continue to function as one flesh, as they did originally. It is the same for us today, as we are also commanded in Genesis 2:24, that when we marry, "the two are to become one flesh" and function as one. His design was perfect and should remain as

He designed it. The dynamic between men and women and their individual purposes and positions are to stay as God intended. The two are to be as one.

Yet, the question still remains: how? How can two people function as one flesh? We are going to more closely examine the original design of mankind and try to answer this question. Today, we are so far away from understanding the dynamics of being one flesh. However, let's not forget that in the beginning, when man and woman were separated, they still understood how to function as one. It wasn't a mystery for them as it is for us today. They knew how to function as one and how to remain as one because they lived it. But for us today, the questions remain: How can two people in two separate bodies function as one entity in unity and harmony? How does the fact that he contained her and she encompassed him play out in our everyday lives? How do two become one, as we are commanded?

I have pondered this picture many times: imagine with me two physical bodies combined into one body. What happens when you have four arms and four legs? You get a clumsy person? Maybe, but that's not really the big problem; you could learn how to use four legs and arms, maybe even more efficiently than two. Two stomachs aren't a major issue. Four kidneys won't slow you down. However, the problems begin with combining two hearts and two minds—of combining two souls. At creation, Father God breathed the breath of lives into mankind and they became two living souls in one flesh. In the last chapter we looked at the definition of the "soul," which is the immaterial part of a person: your mind, your will, and your emotions. The challenge is to imagine combining two wills that stir in different directions and two minds that think completely differently. Imagine trying to combine two sets of emotions and two sets of desires, including all the likes and dislikes and feelings and needs of two separate souls. How is this done? From our unrenewed minds (and our years of experience), we would think that conflict and struggles would be justifiable when trying to combine the two different souls of a man and a woman. However, the reality and the truth is that God did design us to be two souls that function as one. Not only did He design us that way, He commanded us to function that way. As incredible as this is to imagine, we can live today as two souls in perfect unity and harmony.

How can we live this way? We can because we were designed in the very image of God, the image of the Trinity, and there is complete unity in the Trinity. The Trinity consists of three distinct personalities of the Godhead, yet they all are one. For one to speak, they all speak. For one to act, they all act. For one to create, they all create. Though they are three distinct personalities, they are one. The concept of men and women functioning in perfect unity is modeled for us in the Trinity. We have bought into the idea of the power struggle between the sexes because of the errors we have believed about how we were designed and who we are to each other. We have believed the lies. We need to let go of these concepts. We cannot accept the thinking that says that men and women are so different that we cannot have unity. Galatians 3:28 says, "There is neither male nor female; for you are all one in Christ Jesus." This is the truth: ultimately, we are all one in Christ. Male and female were made as two complementary souls that were to function in unity, just as the Trinity.

Today's neurological research supports this concept of a complementary cooperation of the souls. There is much research that explains the differences in men's and women's brains and that supports and reflects the original design of mankind: two personalities with opposite yet equal strengths. It is always thrilling, to me, to see the Word of God being proven by science. Current research shows that we were designed with two different ways of thinking, which complement and complete each other when we think together. These differences are part of God's design. Men and women were created with different ways of thinking; we think best together, because God created mankind to function together, as one flesh.

According to research by the University of Pennsylvania and a published study from Proceedings of the National Academy of Sciences, there are several differences in male and female brains. First of all, they have found that male brains utilize seven times more gray matter, and female brains utilize nearly ten times more white matter. Gray matter is for information and action processing. This is why a man can have a sort of tunnel vision. Due to their ability to focus, once men are engaged in a task, the tunnel vision takes over so that they may not be able to demonstrate much sensitivity to other people. Women having more white matter in their brains helps them to be the encompasser they were designed to be. White matter helps bring information together, making women more able to quickly move from one activity to another, which helps them to be more fluid and flexible. Male and female brains process the same neurochemicals, but they process them differently. The difference in these chemicals causes men to be less inclined to sit still as long as women, and it tends to make them more action-oriented, physically impulsive, and aggressive. Additionally, the way men's brains process chemicals causes them to have less oxytocin than women, which is helpful both for them and for us. This chemical is what allows women to bond with others and to have deep emotional connections more easily than men. Women were made to function best in the internal world of spirit, soul, relationship, and feeling, and the design of our brains reflects that. As the external leader and container, men having fewer deeper emotional connections is a benefit for him. He can decide less emotionally than women and he was wired to act more quickly. Less emotional and quicker responses seem perfect for his position in this leadership team.

We also see God's design in the structural differences between male and female brains. Females have a larger hippocampus and have a higher density of neural connections to the hippocampus. This part of the brain is the memory center, and due to these dense neural connections, women are able to process and absorb more emotional and sensory information than men. Females tend to have better "gut feelings" about things; they sense a lot more of what's going on around them throughout the day, and they retain that information more than men. Again, our design as women is seen in how our brains were created to function. We have brains that pre-wire us to be better equipped than men to function in the internal realm of spirit and soul, exactly where we were designed to live, inside the man.

Additionally, there are significant differences in hemispheres of the brain. These differences in the hemispheres are the cause for our differences in communication. Men tend to be more focused and direct in their communication, while women are less direct. Women can combine verbal information with feeling, emotion, and other sensory information, which may be why women generally have more interest in talking about emotional things. Women have far more blood flow throughout their brain, which causes them to be able to think about and revisit their emotional memories more than men. Men's brain are wired to cause them to reflect differently to emotional information and memories. They tend to analyze them somewhat, and then move on to the next task. During their process, they may choose to change course and do something active and unrelated to feelings rather than to analyze their feelings at all. This is another example of how we function best together. We can supply a man's heart with much needed emotional information that they are lacking, while men can also bring balance to us, keeping us from emotional overload. Some women mistakenly think that men purposefully avoid their feelings or try to solve our problems too quickly. In reality, men are wired that way in order to function as women's counterpart, bringing us balance and providing an opportunity for us to function at our best, just as we also do for them.

Dr. Caroline Leaf is a cognitive neuroscientist and the author of many books including *Who Switched Off My Brain*. From her over twenty-five years of extensive research on the brain, she has come to this conclusion: "Men and women have been created to complement, complete and be compatible with one another through their own unique strengths; we are exponentially better together. He separated our skills so that we must come together to function at our optimum."[23]

Each of our strengths cause us to function best together. Man's ability to compartmentalize his emotions allows him to make more logical and practical decisions and fewer emotional ones, which is perfect for the one who is to "contain" and lead. Women are better at sensing, feeling, intuiting, communicating, and connecting pieces; we naturally tend to understand how the needs of people and circumstances combine. Of course, there are always exceptions; some men are more sensitive and more verbal, and some women are more logical. Some of us have a less polar and more balanced way of thinking. However, for the most part, our brains and how they are wired are what cause men and women to function so differently. As God designed us to, we counterbalance each other. As man's counterpart, his opposite strength, woman was designed to function inside of him. The emotional, intuitional, and internal perspectives that woman supply are important balances to his brain that is wired more toward logic and reason. Together, we create a full, well-rounded perspective. The best decisions are made as a combination of both sets of strengths: men's logical, black-and-white way of thinking and women's intuitive and emotional senses.

This complementary way of thinking is the key to God's view of leadership. Ephesians 5:23 says, "For the husband is the head of the wife as Christ is the head of the church." Consider that the first created male and female were physically in one body, and the male was the only one of the two that had an actual head. Man was built differently from the beginning, and we can understand why men's brains are wired differently than women's. Our original design, as shown in the Word and in science, give understanding to the male's call to lead. He was created to take action and make logical decisions; his brain is best wired for that. Woman was internal; man was external. Woman was in man's chest, and he housed and contained her. He made women to be the inside, the undergird, and the internal; we were created to primarily live in the internal and spiritual realm of the senses. The man had eyes and ears, and he was made to take in information and process things according to logic—what he could see, what he could hear, what was in the physical, etc. God made man to be the literal head, and He also called him to be the spiritual head and to function as the leader within this union. Yet, the call for the man to be a leader is not exclusive; the fact that women are also called to lead is often overlooked.

Women were *also* created to rule and reign, which includes *leading*; however, the *way* women lead differs from men. Looking at the original design, we see that woman was made to be man's equal counterpart; we share the same responsibility to rule and reign. As one being with one shared call, each was to rule and reign and lead in his/her own unique way, yet together, in unity. The woman *internally* led as she influenced the man with her unique perspective. Then, balancing woman's internal influence with his external perspective, the man took action. This is exactly what brain studies have shown us. This is how we are made to function. As dual leaders, with balance and shared perspective, mankind, as both male and female, can rule and reign in unity. Let's not forget that for the first man and woman, in their united leadership and shared perspective, they maintained a burst of creativity so incredible that they, together, named every animal and living thing. Imagine what our world would look like if couples released and maintained the same kind of bursts of creativity today! Creativity that could be used for problem solving, inventing, creating or for finances and business or for any part of life.

The way our brains were designed provides a glimpse into how we function as the encompassers. When woman encompassed man, she functioned as an internal leader with a brain that was wired as such. In this chapter we will continue to bring further definition of what it means to "encompass," and in chapters 2 and 6 we will examine more practical applications of this concept. After looking at our design through the eyes of science, we will now look more closely at the actual word "encompass."

WHAT DOES IT MEAN TO ENCOMPASS?

The Hebrew word for encompass, as found in Strong's Concordance, is H5437, *sabab*. *Sabab* means "to turn about, go around, surround, bring back, circle around, circuit, make a circuit, come around, flow around, surround, turn around, turn, turn aside, come around, engulf."[24] The *Merriam-Webster's Dictionary* defines the word "encompass" as "to form a circle around, surround, encircle, envelop, comprehend."[25] I love how Martin Luther defined it in his commentary on Jeremiah 31:22 — as "an embrace."[26] From these definitions, we see that "encompassing" is truly a position of internal leadership; as we encompass, we influence. Our position is to surround our men, to flow around them with a circuit of energy, to encircle them, and, if needed, to turn them around as we embrace them with the Spirit of God. We are to take all that we sense in the spirit and soul realms and to translate it into influence as we encompass our men's hearts and comprehend them. We turn around what needs to be turned around, and we encircle what needs to be guarded. By looking closely at the definitions of "encompass" and by combining these definitions with the other clues we find in the Word, science, and nature, we get a clearer picture of who we are to our men, we gain more understanding into our design, and we better comprehend how we originally functioned as one flesh.

First, looking more closely at Eve's physical position inside the chest of Adam, in and under his ribs, we see "encompassing" in God's original physical design. We are told that woman was taken from the man's side, most likely from an actual rib or ribs. As we saw in the first chapter, the Hebrew word that is translated as "rib" in Genesis 2 is *tsela*. In other places in the Bible, this word (or its variants) is translated as "side," rather than rib. When he declared that she was "bone of my bone and flesh of my flesh," it may have been a literal statement, indicating that he understood that she was not just from one of his ribs but was also part of his flesh. Since we know that woman was a living soul inside man, she must have had some substance or cell structure. It is quite possible that her cells made up part of his rib bone and part of his flesh, making her literally the flesh and bone of man.

I do believe that is the case: that her cells, her soul, resided in the flesh of his side and in his rib. What does science tell us about ribs? Recent USC research shows that the ribs are filled with stem cells that are able to regenerate.[27] The stem cells in our ribs show us that there is and was potential for the ribs to house the cells of another living soul. Therefore the ribs would be a perfect dwelling place for the cells that contained woman's very soul. It is from this place that woman encompassed man, in the rib cage that surrounds, circles, and embraces him. Not only was she a part of him, she surrounded him, just as the rib cage surrounds him.

What else do we see in the ribs? What other clues are there? In the process of writing this book, I had the unfortunate experience of breaking a rib. In fact, at this moment, every movement I make is painful. The rib cage supports your body at its core, and most of your body's movement is dependent upon your trunk or core (your rib cage), so to speak. If you break a leg or an arm bone, that limb is compromised; however, if you break a rib, your entire body is compromised. You cannot bend, twist, stretch, or lift. It hurts to move your arms, and it hurts to walk. You can't laugh, sneeze, or cough without extreme pain. In fact, you can barely breathe without pain.

Your ribs are the core of every movement you make. In addition to supporting and stabilizing you, your ribs also protect your vital organs. Understanding the ribs helps us understand what the Lord wants to reveal about the original design of woman. Woman lived in the part of man where she could influence him at the core and where she supported his every move. The physical position of woman inside man was one of stabilization, influence, and support. This is a beautiful picture of us as encompassers. *We bring stability to our homes, we bring support to our men, and we set the atmosphere in which everything is sustained.*

Ribs are not only very sensitive bones; they are also some of the few bones in your body that should not be put in a cast when broken. The rib cage needs to keep moving. As you breathe in and out, your ribs are in motion. Your lungs need the freedom to expand and contract; if the rib cage does not expand and contract, the health of your lungs is compromised. I think this is a beautiful picture of who women were created to be to our men. We were in their ribs, surrounding their very life energy, flowing around the deep and vital parts of their being, and moving with them as we allowed them space to breathe. The Holy Spirit also moves, flows, and hovers over us, and we were made in His image. We are in motion as He is: flowing and supporting life.

The original design placed her inside his rib and within his rib cage, surrounding his heart and lungs, and embracing, if you will, his very life. She encompassed: surrounded, encircled, and embraced him at the most vulnerable and the deepest places of his life. In those deep places and with her connection to Father God, woman internally flowed with the Spirit of God around the man. Here, in his ribs, surrounding his inner self, next to the energy center of man, his heart, she flowed around him, and with the Lord, they lived in harmony and peace in the Garden. Proverbs 4:23 tells us, "Guard your heart with all diligence, for from it *flow* the issues of life." The source of your life *flows* from your heart. And woman circled around the flow of man's heart energy, around all the issues of his life. He now could understand his internal self on a deeper level as she flowed around him, completing the circuit with the Spirit of God and life. In this position inside man and near his heart, we see woman created to be a part of the internal flow that is coming from the heart of man. Here is woman; this is where she dwells and flows, perceives and senses, circles, supports and influences the very heart of man.

In this picture, we can also see the concept of "circuit, make a circuit," which is also part of meaning of *sabab*. This is a beautiful picture of what it was like for woman to live inside the chest of man. She flowed as a circuit of energy that literally surrounded, encircled, and encompassed his heart. That energy flowed from heart to mind, from heart to spirit, and from spirit to spirit. Again, here is the image of the Trinity. The energy of God flows within the Trinity. The Lord is a Spirit, and the Spirit is an energy. It is the function of the Holy Spirit as He releases the miraculous power and energy of God. He appeared as tongues of fire at Pentecost, with a mighty rushing wind. He is the one who releases energy where and how the Father commands. This same energy created the world and all that's in it; it brings healing and deliverance and salvation to all people; it opens eyes and minds and hearts. The Holy Spirit moves as a flow of energy; and we read that "out of your innermost being shall flow rivers of living water" (John 7:38). As women encompass or make a circle around their men, they too make circuits of energy. Women set the atmosphere, and what exactly is atmosphere but a tone, a mood, a vibe, a spiritual ambience, an energy. In the likeness of the Holy Spirit, women were designed with the ability to flow around man as a circle of energy and life—an electric impulse of the energy of God.

Similarly, women function in the internal world of spirit, soul, thought, and feeling as the Holy Spirit also functions. This is our domain, in a like manner to the Holy Spirit. Second Corinthians 2:10–12 says, "For to us God revealed them through the Spirit; for the Spirit searches all things, even the depths of God. For who among men knows the thoughts of a man except the spirit of the man which is in him? Even so, the thoughts of God no one knows except the spirit of God." This passage shows us that members of the Trinity relate to each other and something of how they relate. We see from this passage that the Holy Spirit can and does relate *internally* with the Father God. The Holy Spirit is the only one who searches the very thoughts that rest within the heart of the Father. This is the picture of "encompassing" within the Trinity; here the Holy Spirit encompasses the heart of the Father. It is the Holy Spirit who knows the thoughts of God. How this happens is a mystery to me, but I do know that in the same way the Holy Spirit flows inside the heart of the Father, the female was designed to flow around the heart of the male. Like the Holy Spirit in the Trinity, woman can internally sense and understand a man. In the same way the Holy Spirit searches the deep places of the Father, women encompass the deep places of their man.

Woman was designed to dwell in the rib cage that surrounds the heart and the lungs and the spirit of man. The ribs surround the life-supporting systems of the hearts and lungs. Even more importantly, the ribs surround the spiritual and emotional center of the man. Woman lived close to man's spirit and the deep parts of his immaterial being. In the Word we see that the spirit of man, our inward man, sits at what is described as the "kidneys," or the "cloud layers." These layers are the layers of our inward being (see Psalm 51:6; Job 38:36). Woman surrounded the layers of man's internal man. This is a beautiful picture of the word "encompass" and its meaning of to *embrace*. I love how God uses such simple things to teach us and show us such profound lessons.

Today's amazing research regarding the heart, its energy field, and the way the heart interacts with the brain further demonstrates what it means to encompass. Again, science is helping us interpret this concept of who we are as women. According to the HeartMath Research Institute, the heart and brain maintain a continuous two-way dialogue, each influencing the other's functioning. The heart sends signals to the brain that can influence perception, emotional processing, and higher cognitive functions. This system is referred to as "heart brain" by neurocardiology researchers. What is really fascinating is that the heart contains a "brain" in its own right. The human heart, in addition to its other functions, actually possesses a heart-brain composed of about forty thousand neurons that can sense, feel, learn, and remember. The heart-brain sends messages to the head brain about how the body feels and more. Here again is the place for woman, the encompasser, who surrounds the heart of man. In the original design, she influenced him here and became a part of, an influence in, and a guard for his thinking and reasoning and all the issues of his life. Women can again hold this position.[21]

Also, according to HeartMath, our heart is the largest source of energy in our body. Scripture tells us that all of our life flows from our hearts; said another way, the energy of life flows from our hearts. As we were made in the image of God, who is energy, we were made to create and emit energy, too, as we "encompass," flow around and make a circuit that surrounds the heart of man. This is powerful and profound. In the next chapter, we will look at the fall of man that occurred when the female brought a circuit of the wrong energy to the male. For now, here are some more interesting facts from HeartMath that we can apply to this concept of encompassing: The heart is the most powerful generator of electromagnetic energy in the human body, and it is sixty times greater than the brain's energy field. The heart's powerful electromagnetic field can be detected and measured from several feet away from a person's body and can be sensed between two individuals in close proximity. The data from HeartMath research showed that when people touch or are close to one another, a transference occurs of the electromagnetic energy produced by the heart. It not only transfers to others; it is also magnetic. Like the electromagnetic energy of the Trinity, it draws you in. As the Lord draws us unto Himself, we all, men and women, have that same ability to draw in others. Women, specifically, were designed to dwell near the heart, near the most electrically powerful part of a man's physical body. We flowed around his heart and surrounded the electromagnetic energy it released. We have been designed with this ability to create and shift atmosphere (which is energy).[28] We can and do bring energy to our men and can sense the energy around them and our families. We can connect others to the circuit of the flow of life-giving energy.[29] We do not know how powerful we are!

The multilayered term "flow" or "flows around" is used throughout this book. It is a powerful concept that also reflects the Trinity and the Holy Spirit. The Holy Spirit flows around creation and all created beings. In a similar way, women release a flow of the Spirit. We were created to flow around our men, our families, and our homes, with the internal and intangible things of life. We flow around them with prayer, with joy, with peace, and with the presence of the Lord and the Word of God. Women are responsible for making sure these things keep flowing in our relationships with our husbands and keep flowing around their hearts. We, as women, set the tone; we create the atmosphere. In today's language, the common saying, "If Mamma ain't happy, no one's happy," reflects this concept. For now, suffice it to say that we women were designed to flow around our men, our marriages, our families, and our homes with intangible (and sometimes physical) things that work together to create atmosphere. We can see this idea in scientific findings regarding our brains, which were wired for the easy flow of information regarding intuition, feelings, and internal perceptions. That is the original design and this is where God is taking us!

Another important part of the word "encompass" includes to turn around, to turn about, or to cause to change direction. There's a cliché in today's culture that says, "Men are the head and women are the neck; we turn the head wherever we wish." I see a hint of our original design in that saying; women were designed to help men "turn around" or "cause to change direction" when they're headed in the wrong direction. It is clear that the man was created with an actual head. Woman may not have been created with a physical head like man, but women do hold the power to turn that head. Woman dwelled somewhere in the rib cage, which, again, is the part of the body that supports and directs movement. From our position in the rib, and from the definition of "encompass" we see that woman was designed to influence and even create movement from her internal position. From these concepts, it is clear that we encompass by helping our men to see (from our internal influence) and we have the ability to move them toward the right direction (as we did in their rib). This is what we are capable of being to our men and what we were designed to do; we are internal leaders who hold a position of power, and we have a value that far exceeds being a helper who simply keeps man from being lonely. We will talk more about "turning around" in a later chapter.

Everything we've looked at so far, combined together, gives us a picture of the original design of women as encompassers. We were created with a strong ability to live in an internal and spiritual place. We were created to be intuitive, emotional, and relational. We were created as souls to comfortably live in the internal world. Our brains were designed to function best at sensing, discerning, and understanding. We were originally designed to live in an internal space that surrounded and guarded the important, life-giving organs of the male as well as his heart, soul and spirit. We were created to be the influencers, stabilizers, and supporters of our men. Bringing all of these abilities as the *ezer kennegdo*—we bring these strengths as man's counterpart, the one who fights alongside him, his equal but opposite strength that balances him. This is who we were made to be.

We help man by surrounding him as his support and encouragement.

We help by circling him and making a circuit of the energy of God around him.

We bring our voice with our different yet complementary perceptions and thoughts.

We fight alongside him with the energy of God as we flow around him with God's power.

We guard his heart and all that flows from it with our prayers and emotional support.

We draw him into the right flow of God, and if he needs us to, we fight to turn him around and turn him back.

We bring valuable insights that we sense from the Spirit of God.

We create life-filled and love-filled atmosphere charged with the energy of God.

Woman was designed to encompass. She dwelled in the ribs that supported him, surrounded him, and protected his life-giving organs and the life of his inward man. She dwelled in the rib cage that circled, embraced, and supported him at the very core of his being. As his equal-strength counterpart, she supplied to him what he needed in his internal world, and she gave him a valued and much-needed perspective that was different from his own. She communicated with him in the deepest parts of his heart. She was his equal-but-opposite strength counterpart who supported him physically, emotionally, and spiritually. She led internally as he led externally. She led with her ability to influence, with her internal knowing, and with her intuition as she flowed around him in a circuit of God's energy. She brought to him the energy of God, of life. She was the source and the flow of life-giving energy to him at his very core. She would set the atmosphere in and around them, protect it, and circle him and their union, with the life-giving, life-sustaining energy of God. She would keep this circuit of life flowing around them as they took dominion, ruled and reigned over everything they were responsible for with creativity, power, unity and the energy of life.

This is where we can live today. Women can live from this place of incredible *influence* and *power*, in the deepest places in the hearts of men. Woman is at her best in the world of internal, intangible, and immaterial. We women were designed to lead internally, in the unseen world of spirit, of energy, and of atmosphere. We can influence the hearts of men and mankind and we can influence our men and mankind from within their hearts. History gives us some examples of men being influenced and inspired by women; men have built amazing buildings, have founded great companies, have made important discoveries and amassed fortunes all because of the inspiration of a woman. This is who we are and what we can do for men. God did not intend for just a few women to be powerful, inspiring examples; *all* women have this power available every day. God wants you to be the energy, the inspiration, and the source of life to your man. This is women's design, and this is what we are taking back. We can create a culture where women are honored and valued for being the much needed inspiration to men, where men can become their best selves and take their place as powerful leaders and creators.

Unfortunately, what we have seen for thousands of years, in every generation and in every culture, is that women have lived from a different position—the position we assumed after the Fall. Even so, God is revealing His truth in order to heal us, not to shame us. In this next chapter, we will look at how we lost our original position, how that continued, and we will find new hope in how we *can* and *will* recapture our powerful place.

3

THE FALL OF MANKIND

> "I've learned a lot about women. I think I've learned exactly how the fall of man occurred in the Garden of Eden. Adam and Eve were in the Garden of Eden, and Adam said one day, 'Wow, Eve, here we are, at one with nature, at one with God, we'll never age, we'll never die, and all our dreams come true the instant that we have them.' And Eve said, 'Yeah... it's just not enough is it?'"
> ‖ BILL HICKS, AMERICAN COMEDIAN[30]

In Genesis 2:17, the Lord told Adam and Eve, "But you must not eat from the tree of the knowledge of good and evil, for when you eat from it, you will certainly die." Not maybe, but certainly. Strong words for Mankind! At this point of the story, mankind was together, with the Father, in perfect unity and harmony, naked and unashamed. Genesis 2 ends with mankind separated into two bodies yet still functioning as one flesh, in peaceful unity ruling the planet with the Father. Yet even in this beautiful picture of unity among man, woman, and God, vulnerability still existed. Even in this perfect, pristine environment, the female was drawn into temptation.

I have looked at this part of the story so many times, wondering why would she do it? Ultimately, Eve took and ate from that tree because she was human. As hard as that is to accept, it is the truth: mankind is vulnerable. Our flesh, our free will, and our human nature: this is the vulnerability that the Enemy uses to tempt, trap, and sometimes defeat us. In her human nature, Eve allowed her flesh to be tempted. She was deceived into thinking that she needed something more (see 1 Timothy 2:13). It is said so well in the quote that opened this chapter, though it was meant in jest, it still contains some truth. The truth was that, for whatever reason, the perfect world she lived in just wasn't enough for her. Her flesh wanted more, and because she was human, she had the same vulnerability and the same desires of the flesh that we do. First John 2:16 spells out for us the very human condition that was part of mankind from the beginning: "The lust of the flesh, the lust of the eyes, the boastful pride of life, is not of the Father" (KJV). Eve *saw* the fruit, and even though it was *not* of the Father, she desired it. It looked good, and she believed it could make her wise. She took it, and she tasted it. It tasted good, and she brought it to Adam. She brought it to him because that was *exactly* what she was *designed* to do; she was designed to encompass, influence, and flow around him. As soon as she decided to have this new and exciting thing, she wanted to bring that to him too; she wanted to bring him what was so delicious and filling; she wanted to flow toward him with the new energy she had opened herself to. She was functioning from her design, encompassing him.

The reality is that the Enemy of all mankind knows how we are made; he understands God's original design and he knew how to manipulate that design to get what he wanted. The Enemy had his target set on having all the authority and the control of the planet. He knew that in order to get that authority and control, *both* man and woman had to surrender it because he knew that they were each one half of a whole and therefore they must *act as one*. The Enemy had to get *both* of them to choose and act *together* to eat that fruit. The easiest way for him to get them both to act was to go through the *woman*, the one who was created to *encompass* the man's heart with the power to *influence*. He could then use the woman's power of influence to lure the man to the trap. The Enemy exploited their very design to overtake them. His snare to take them down was fashioned with their design and their

THE FALL OF MANKIND

strengths and weaknesses as humans in mind. His strategy was simple but very effective. Use the influencer to influence while appealing to the flesh—a two-edged sword.

There they were in the garden, standing at the very tree they were not supposed to eat from. Genesis 3:6 says, "So when the woman saw that the tree was good for food, that it was pleasant to the eyes, and a tree desirable to make one wise, she took of its fruit and ate. She also gave to her husband with her and he ate" (NKJV). She gave in to the lust of her flesh, the lust of her eyes, and the pride of life. She let her flesh take over, and she ate. *Then she did exactly as she was designed to do: she encompassed the man, just as the Enemy knew she would do.* She turned to the man, her counterpart, and using her abilities to influence and create circuits of energy, she handed him the fruit. Until this point, mankind had lived in oneness with the Spirit of God. Woman had flowed around them with the life energy of God, and man had lead them. They had lived as one—naked, safe in their vulnerability, and unashamed, surrounded by the glory of God. Now the woman had *death* in her hand and she offered it to the man. She encompassed him and now it was his turn to decide and act. It is important to remember man's position and strengths: he was designed to contain woman, to protect her, and to lead them. When woman brought man the fruit, it was his time to function from his position. He was designed to *contain* her, and part of the definition of "containing" is to *restrain the spread of something that is potentially harmful*. In this case, man needed to contain the threat of sin and death. As the leader and protector, part of his job was to protect woman, their oneness and the planet. As the man, the container, he was to decide if his encompasser was bringing to him something of God or not. If not, his job was to contain the danger and protect them both and their environment. As the external leader, he was to lead them away from what was evil or harmful so they could remain in the presence of God and in their perfect environment.

Both man and woman made choices from their fleshly nature and using the free will that they were created with as human beings. Their human flesh was a point of weakness for both of them, and the enemy trapped them with it, while using their design against them. Woman made choices from the lust of her flesh: the fruit looked good, she wanted it, her flesh desired it. She made the choice for that fruit—for its new and powerful flow—and she brought this new thing that she had lusted for to the man. She was now encompassing him from her flesh instead of with and from the Spirit. Man allowed himself to be tempted with what she was bringing him. His flesh overtook him, too. He failed to do his job as the godly, life-sustaining "container," and he failed to at least examine what the woman had introduced to him. Our flesh will consistently take the easy route, the path of least resistance, the lazy way. She influenced him, and he, in lazy resignation, took the bait. He failed the ultimate test of leadership. In Genesis 3:17, God condemns Adam "because you *listened* to the voice of your wife." In Hebrew, this word "listened" means "obeyed." Adam did not just listen to Eve; he obeyed her. He did not obey *God*; instead he chose to obey *Eve* and he did not do his job as protector, container, and leader.

They gave into their flesh. It is now their humanness, the flesh, that is at work in their design. She has stepped away from the Spirit of God and instead has a new spirit at work within her. She is not encompassing him from the Spirit of God and life but from the lust of her flesh. This is the power of our design and the example for us as women: when we flow and encompass with our flesh or from the power of the Enemy, there are powerful consequences set in motion.

Next to happen is the first of many consequences, and it is very profound. If you look closely at the story, you see that as soon as *he* ate, their eyes were opened. Not before. This didn't happen when *she* ate—only when *he* ate. Genesis 3:6–7 says, "She also gave to her husband with her and he ate. *Then* the eyes of *both* of them were opened" (NKJV, italics added for emphasis). This is very important to understand and accept. She ate the fruit and nothing happened. Both of their eyes were opened only when the two acted together—when the man received from her and accepted. They were one, so they chose as one and acted as one, with him being the final authority, as the designated leader. I wonder what would have happened if man would have chosen to do the harder work of "containing" her in the original way he was designed, the Spirit-filled design, not the flesh-filled design. He could have said, "What you have brought to us is not of God; we will not eat this." He could have taken her to the Father, presented her to Him and said, "Please help us. We have done what is not right. Forgive this and wash this away from us, from my *ezer kennegdo*, my counter-part, who has made a mistake in what she has chosen and encompassed me with." If he had functioned properly in his position as the protector/container/leader and had taken her before the Father, there would not have been a Fall, and death would not have been released on this planet. They would have been preserved from death and would have remained blameless. This is what God still commands men today: to wash their wives with the Word and to present them to the Lord as blameless and without blemish (see Ephesians 5:26). Yet, that is not what happened during the Fall. Man did not contain woman, nor did he present her as blameless. Instead, he blamed her completely, as we see later in the story. Yet if the man had made a better choice, if he had not given in to his flesh too, death would not have touched them, and their eyes would not have been opened. Remember, nothing happened until they both ate. Once they both ate, then and only then were their eyes opened. This immediate consequence not only gives us more understanding to their design, but we see the power in it.

One of our definitions of "encompass" was "to make a circuit." We see this in action during their fall: woman literally carried an energy that created a *circuit* when man accepted and received it. In order to make an electrical circuit and release a flow of energy, there must be a receiving end; otherwise the energy won't flow, and the circuit will remain unconnected or broken. When man received the fruit and ate it, when he connected the circuit that woman had encompassed him with, he completed that circuit. Energy was released and flowed through them. Unfortunately, the woman had encompassed him with an energy that would introduce death to them and the planet. Again, as she created a circuit of this energy, that death energy was not actually *released* until Adam *received it*, in the same way that all electrical circuits work. When the circuit was completed, the energy of death was released. The first thing death energy did was to open their eyes. Just as when you plug in the lamp and the light goes on energy was released and their eyes opened. Originally, only *life* energy covered the planet,: there was Mankind and the glorious presence of God; they were in full control of the planet; there was no death; there was only life. Now death, through sin, came to the planet with this circuit connection. Death became active in their world and the first thing it did was immediately open their eyes. What did it open their eyes to? Guilt, fear and shame, which drove them to hide from their Father God. At this moment, because of their choices, death touched mankind, overtook the planet, and brought corruption to everything: all of this destruction stemming from the choices they made, from their flesh, *through* their powerful design.

Romans 5:17 says, "Therefore just as sin entered the world through one man, and death through sin, in this way death came to all people." This death energy ignited immediate change not only in mankind but also in the planet. Death became a veil that covered the planet (see 1 Corinthians 15:21) and stretched out over all. Man and woman released death. Now "the shadow of

THE FALL OF MANKIND

death...hangs over the Earth" (Isaiah 25:7). The *New Living Translation* says it this way: "[death is] the covering cast over the people, the veil that is spread over the Earth." This veil or canopy of sin/death energy is now covering this planet. It came when, together, as one, mankind released death, and death brought corruption. God's first creation—which was made in His image to walk in unity, power, and authority and which was intended to create, rule, multiply, and release Him and His glory on this planet—fell. This power couple lost everything and released sin and death over the entire planet. The Enemy defeated them and got what he wanted: the authority and control of the planet. In exploiting their design and appealing to their flesh, the Enemy gained access to the planet. The original design of mankind was compromised, and the dynamic between them was corrupted.

We are now at a critical part of the story, which has also been misinterpreted for generations. What actually happens to man and woman now? What are mankind's actual consequences? They are not what we have previously believed. In Genesis 3:14–21 God explains how death has changed the relationship between man and woman and how they function together:

> *"And Jehovah God said unto the serpent, Because thou hast done this, cursed art thou above all cattle, and above every beast of the field; upon thy belly shalt thou go, and dust shalt thou eat all the days of thy life: and I will put enmity between thee and the woman, and between thy seed and her seed: he shall bruise thy head, and thou shalt bruise his heel. Unto the woman he said, I will greatly multiply thy pain and thy conception; in pain thou shalt bring forth children; and thy desire shall be to thy husband, and he shall rule over thee. And unto Adam he said, Because thou hast hearkened unto the voice of thy wife, and hast eaten of the tree, of which I commanded thee, saying, Thou shalt not eat of it: cursed is the ground for thy sake; in toil shalt*

> *thou eat of it all the days of thy life; thorns also and thistles shall it bring forth to thee; and thou shalt eat the herb of the field; in the sweat of thy face shalt thou eat bread, till thou return unto the ground; for out of it wast thou taken: for dust thou art, and unto dust shalt thou return. And the man called his wife's name Eve; because she was the mother of all living. And Jehovah God made for Adam and for his wife coats of skins, and clothed them."*
> —Genesis 3:14–21, ASV

Death and corruption came to man and woman, which created consequences, not "curses." The idea of mankind being cursed is another commonly accepted concept, however, God actually never curses them. God only uses the word "cursed" when talking to the Devil and regarding the ground; He does not use that word when addressing man and woman. We are His beloved creation, created in His image, and He has blessed us not cursed us. Are there consequences to their sins? Yes, but not curses. This is more than a difference in semantics; as we shall see, the relationship consequences she receives provide more validation to mankind's true design. What does happen is that God curses the Enemy and then He turns to the woman and says, basically, that death has touched her and that she will experience consequences. One of those consequences is the change of the relationship dynamic. He explains the new relationship pattern, "Your desire shall be for your husband and he shall rule over you" (NKJV). He *then* turns to the man and tells him that the *ground* is cursed and that now work is hard for him because of the curse on the ground. He tells man that because of what he did, in releasing sin and death, mankind will decay and die and one day return to the dust they came from. Both the man and the woman face consequences for their choice to sin. These consequences for each of them affect the other, and all mankind, and the results of these consequences are staggering.

THE FALL OF MANKIND

Mankind's entire design, which was based on the peaceful flow of God's Spirit between them, is corrupted and compromised. What was once a relationship filled with unity, based on complement, has been changed to a whole new pattern. Before we look in detail at their corrupted dynamic and how this new relationship will function, let's further consider who man and woman were to each other and what God had revealed to them before the Fall. From the time they were created until the Fall, God had shown or told man and woman, "You are equal counter-parts that together are mankind. You are opposites but the same—two complementary yet different parts of the same whole. You were created to encompass and respond, to function uniquely as two distinct and different parts, yet in unity, because you are one entity." *Man and woman acted and functioned as one flesh in tandem with each other and with God's Spirit.* Mankind had unbroken access and fellowship with Him; they were surrounded with the atmosphere of God, and His presence was with them and around them. They had God's Presence and life Spirit breathed into them at creation, and they flowed in and with it. Together, they carried God's image and acted as one, like the Trinity. But when they chose death over life, death entered the planet, their relationship with God, and their relationship with each other. There is much to look at in this, and there is much to grieve and to recover. (This book, however, will primarily focus on Eve and on what happened to the male/female relationship.)

THE CONSEQUENCES OF THE FALL

First of all, I want to make this very clear: the consequences to the male and female relationship were placed on the *woman* and the man receives of this consequence but by *default*. This is important because it helps to explain their design. After the Fall, the woman was told, "Your desire will be for him, and he will rule over you." God did not say to her, "Your desire will be for him," and *then* turn to the man to say, "Your consquence is that you will rule over her." No, *God only addressed the woman*, saying that the new pattern is that she would desire after him *and* he would rule over her. Her consequence is a new relationship; it's going to be different! Why was this new relationship pattern, or dynamic, a consequence given to her and not given to him? Because the woman was designed as the encompasser. She was designed with the responsibility to flow life over the relationship, to surround man at the deepest parts of his being and to encompass them and their relationship with the Spirit of life. She was designed to start the flow and he was designed to respond. She set the tone, started the flow and was a sort of "keeper of the relationship," this was her part of this team, called mankind. The weight of their relationship fell on her and so the weight of the consequence fell on her too. Here we clearly see that her consequences from the Fall actually *confirm* their design. She was told that man would *respond* to her differently as she will now encompass him with "desire after him." His response will be "ruling over her." Same design, different flow.

The Lord never changed the design of mankind; that is still intact. Death and corruption did not change our design. Man and woman still were and are a being that functions in tandem, designed to be a one-flesh leadership team. However, the design was compromised by the corruption that came from death. After the Fall, the design of planet Earth didn't *change*; there was gravity, and oceans and seed time and harvest, even though the Earth was corrupted from sin and death. The ground was cursed, but the design of it remained; the dirt would continue to produce vegetation, a lesser quality, perhaps, and it would require more work from man to produce it, but the design was the same. The design of woman and man, encompasser and container, as a two-part leadership team, was still intact. Woman is still the encompasser. Man is still the container. That has not changed.

We are still designed to function as one flesh. However, the flow of life, the blessings of oneness, and the power of their oneness have been compromised. The new dynamic in this two-part team is that she will *encompass* by desire after him and he will *respond* with ruling over her. She will no longer encompass him with life and he will not respond back as the life-filled container of woman. Yet, as the encompasser she is still the spark, the impetus, the catalyst.

This is why the Lord is seeking to restore women to our original position. We have the ability to change our relationship with and to men because that is our design. Even though the corrupted dynamic *started* with us and it was us who set in the motion the compromise of original design, it also can *end* with us. We can be the catalyst for *restoration*. This will be further discussed in more detail in a later chapter. For now let's hold on to that hope as we look more closely at the corrupted dynamic.

THE DYNAMICS OF THEIR CORRUPTED RELATIONSHIP

God basically told Eve, "Here is the new dynamic: woman will now have an intense desire for man." Depending on the translation you read, it may say desire *after* or a desire *for* men. Instead of encompassing man with life and the Spirit of God, woman now encompasses him with a *desire* for him. What does this mean? In the original Hebrew text, this phrase "desire after" is *tĕshuwqah* (H8669).[31] This term translates as "desire, intense craving, longing." It comes from a root word that means "to stretch out after." This word *tĕshuwqah* is found *only three times* in the entire Bible, and only twice is it translated exactly as in Genesis 3:17—as an "intense craving" or an "intense desire" for something. The same wording used in Genesis 3:17 is repeated a chapter later in Genesis 4:7. The third time this "desire after" phrase is used is in Song of Solomon, where it has a slightly different meaning.

Here is a breakdown of the three instances:

> 1. Genesis 3:16: "*Your desire will be* for your husband, and he will rule over you" (NIV, emphasis added). Women are now going to intensely crave and long for a man. A woman will desire and need a man, deeply and intensely. She will forever stretch out after a man. Women will intensely crave man the same way we see sin craves us, in the second appearance of this word.
>
> 2. Genesis 4:7: "If you do what is right, will you not be accepted? But if you do not do what is right, sin is crouching at your door; *it desires to have you*, but you must rule over it" (NIV, emphasis added). In Genesis 4:7, God is telling Cain to watch out for sin because sin intensely craves and longs for him. Sin desires to have him. Sin brought death, and death is an energy that, in this verse, wants and desires Cain very intensely. These two verses are giving us the same picture of "desiring after."
>
> 3. Song of Solomon 7:10 reads, "I belong to my beloved, and *his desire is for me*" (NIV, emphasis added). Though this is a book written between two lovers, Solomon and his bride, yet we can also interpret this book as a love letter from our God to us. We hear Him in this love letter to us, as the One who loves us so intensely that He desires after us, to have relationship with us. It is Him who longs for us. He wants to overtake us in His love. In the Hebrew text the root word for "*desire after*" is the same but has a slightly different variation of that word. In this passage, God is giving us a new picture of what pure longing is.

It is a longing that comes from the desire to give and not get, to connect with us, rather than a desire that wants to possess us.

In all three uses, the connotation is strong: longing, craving, stretching out after, desiring. These words have one definition in common: the intense or passionate wanting of something. Both "longing" and "stretching out after" insinuate a craving for something that is out of reach, never to be completely captured. When I crave something, it is all I can think about. My mind dwells on it, my heart yearns for it, and I am distracted from other things as what I crave becomes my focus. The consequence of woman's sin is that she will focus on, long after, intensely crave, and passionately want man. She will be filled with an intense need and will "long after" and "stretch herself to reach for" a man, and man will become her focus.

Mankind was made to desire the Lord. We are to delight ourselves in Him (see Psalm 37:4), and we are to love nothing else or anyone else more than Him (see Exodus 20:3). He is to be our everything. We are to seek Him and only Him, first, and with all our hearts (see Mark 12:30). If woman is to "intensely crave" someone or something, it is to be God. If she is to need anything or anyone, it is to be Him. Now, because of the corruption of her design, woman encompasses man with a desire for him. Remember, her design didn't changed; it was just corrupted. Woman is still the encompasser, but now she encompasses man with her intense need for him. More on this subject in the following chapters, but for now we will focus on the truth that the corrupted dynamic is in place; woman lost her connection to God and instead intensely craves man.

Mankind must have experienced a period of grieving as they realized all they had lost. They lost their relationship with and their access to the Father, they lost their home, their purpose, they lost their natural life, their unity, they lost their authority, they lost their power and position, they lost their identity, they lost their innocence, and more and more. They were alone in their pain. I cannot imagine the depth of that grief. I can think of my own times of loss and deep pain: losing a child, losing my home, losing my marriage to a man I deeply loved. As much as I can say that these were soul-crushing times of grief for me, they didn't happen all at once and they are small in comparison to all that this couple lost in one day. They lost everything in one moment. What the Lord has shown me is, at this point, the pain of an orphan settled deep into their broken lives and hearts. Deep in their very cells, they carried the pain of an orphan who was full of abandonment and rejection.

They were rejected from the Garden and separated from the Father. Just as anyone who has been orphaned, they were filled with deep pain.

This is not what the Father wanted for His first created children. This was not His perfect plan. They, together, made choices that resulted in their abandonment and loss. This hurt the Father, too. He lost His children, and He knew the cost of His plan to heal and redeem and restore them as His children. Man and woman felt the pain of the death they embraced. At their core was no longer life but death and the pain of it. There was a new identity for them. They became orphans on a corrupted planet over which they no longer had authority.

This pain fueled the corrupted dynamic of men and women. This couple who at one time lived as close as two people could be—her living inside him in perfect unity—became orphaned, abandoned, fractured, and rejected. They experienced shame, regret, fear, and guilt. Yet the greatest loss was that of their relationship with the Father. Death touched the core of woman's being and filled her with abandonment and rejection and a host

THE FALL OF MANKIND

of other emotions. No longer did the life-giving Spirit of God surround her. This loss and this pain fueled her craving and intense need for a man. It is from this new "spirit" that she encompassed Adam, this spirit or atmosphere of "need." No longer did she encompass him with the Spirit of God. Mankind's connection to the Father was lost, and they did not have the Holy Spirit flowing inside them nor were they surrounded by His presence, as they were in the garden. What they did have was the pain of a rejected, abandoned orphan, looking for relief. *It is the craving of an orphan that overtakes her design to encompass and fuels her "intense craving" for man.*

These deep emotions became the fuel for her craving for man: the deep pain of fear, shame, guilt, and the pain of insecurity. Insecurity came to the heart of mankind when they fell. Insecurity says, "I am scared," "I need you," "I'm unsure of my identity," and "I am not enough." Man's and woman's identity had been with each other and with the Father. They were two parts of the same whole; there was a security that said, "We are one. We belong. We are a part of each other and a part of the Father." They both had security, and for the woman, because she was created inside him and was contained by him as a part of him, she had security *in* him. The security she had in that position was gone, compromised by sin and death. When she lost her connection with the Father and then with Adam, she was no longer sure of her own position as an individual.

Woman's craving after, her desire for, and her longing for a man resulted from her lost identity and the empty vacuum of her broken heart. The pain of abandonment, rejection, insecurity, and shame caused her to cry out for relief. What we see in the Genesis 3:17 passage is *not* that the Lord cursed her for being a "bad girl" for eating from the tree and He did *not* "curse" her for disobeying Him. What we really hear is that with a sad heart, the Lord said to her, "Death has touched your soul, and there are consequences to that. You are going to hurt. You do not have the same access to Me and because I cannot touch your heart as I could before, you are going to look for relief in your man. You are going to surround him with an intense craving and you will long for and yearn for him to fill you." From this time forward, in every generation, woman began to emotionally crave man, looking to him to comfort her grieving, abandoned, and rejected self. She needed him, emotionally and spiritually. She lost her spiritual fullness with the Father and felt an empty vacuum of spiritual need. She was filled with pain and hurt, and it began to control her. No longer did she encompass man with the Spirit of God; instead she encompassed him with her need for him, fueled by her pain. This is what the intense craving or desiring after a man looks like.

As we have seen, the original design for women is still present, but it has been compromised. The powerful ability given to women to encompass, to influence, and to internally lead was fueled from the life-giving energy of the Spirit of God. We were made to flow around men with life, and now we flow around them in our need. Now, we encompass and surround them with our intense craving for them, and in return, they respond to our need by ruling over us. Genesis 3:16 says, "Your desire will be for your husband, and *he will rule over you*." The Lord says the man has no choice but to respond to us, because we were created to function in tandem. Woman encompasses man with a circuit of energy, and he responds to it; this is the design. His response is different because she flows around him with something different. Her internal leadership and influence have become need-driven and selfish; that is the fuel or the spirit that she will now encompass with. He no longer responds as the container/leader/protector; instead he contains her like an *oppressor*, and he responds to her flow of need with a desire to *rule over* her. He was designed to "contain" her as in protect, keep, and hold her and yet he is *still* the container of woman. However, the way he contains is corrupted. The word "contain" also means stifle, subdue, repress, and control! This is the new flow of the relationship. They have the same design, but now it is compromised and the dynamic is corrupted. She "intensely craves him" and his response is to "rule over" her; she *encompasses* him with her need, her pain, and he *contains* her with subduing, repressing, stifling, and controlling.

This perspective of the Fall of man is far from the accepted church teachings that I have heard over and over. We have all heard the idea that at the Fall, man and woman were cursed, that her curse was that she would "desire" him, meaning that she would want control; she would want to be in charge and fight him for leadership and that he would be the leader. Is that really our "curse"? No! The Lord does not say to Eve that she is cursed with a desire to be in charge. In fact, He doesn't say that she is cursed at all.

THE LAW OF FIRST MENTION

Remember the Law of First Mention? It teaches us to build understanding upon the simplest foundation. Let's apply that law to the Christian church's commonly held doctrine regarding the creation of Mankind. First we would begin with the error that only the male was made in God's image, as the Man in Charge of the Planet, and that woman was made as his assistant. Next, we would add the error that mankind was cursed at the Fall with a fight for control. From these two errors we would thereby set the foundation for man and woman to have inequality, and never-ending conflicts and power struggles, unless, of course, the woman just shut up and got in her place beneath man.

If we accept these errors, then we would be unable to truly explain much about why mankind fell and the results from that fall. Why did the Enemy begin with the woman? Why didn't he go directly to the man? Why did the woman bring the man the fruit? Why didn't the woman's eyes open when she ate? Why did *both* their eyes open when *he* ate? Why was woman the only one to receive the consequence to the relationship? There are so many unanswered questions. If we believe the incorrect assumption that they received curses for their bad behavior and that woman's curse was that man would be in charge and she would fight him for it, then we get far away from who man and woman truly are to each other. If we built on these errors, we would certainly not understand the consequences beyond seeing that there is a power struggle between man and woman, created at the Fall, with no motive other than a desire for control. This belief gives us no insight into questions of why or who or how! (Think of how these mindsets affect our understanding of submission.) This view doesn't account for woman's contribution to mankind's call to rule and reign together, nor does it make sense according to the rest of scripture. This view gives us no insight into who man and woman are to each other. We have no understanding about their powerful design.

When we build our understanding of what happened at the Fall with our foundational truths about the true original design of mankind, then we can easily understand and apply truth about their consequences. The original design was of two complementary, equal-power individuals that functioned in complete unity as one. Woman was designed to internally influence and lead; she was to maintain the flow of the Spirit of God around man, and man was to respond by containing, protecting, and leading. She then chose death and, in her design, encompassed and influenced man with this wrong spirit. Because he, Adam, did not do his job to protect and lead, because he listened to her influence, he received death from her, therefore, *together* they fell and lost everything. They lost all their authority and power and they opened the door for sin, death and corruption. This is the more accurate picture of what happened. From this foundation, we apply these truths to their consequences at the Fall.

The encompasser was compromised. The influencer became the manipulator; the supportive sustainer became needy and demanding. The *ezer kennegdo*, who was designed to fight with him as his opposite strength will now fight against him as an opposite, an opponent. The one who flowed around man with life now flows with the pains of death. Instead of flowing to him, she now craves him, and he will never completely fill her craving. She will desire to have his heart; she will no longer support and guard it. She needs his heart because she lost her relationship with and connection to the Father's heart. Her position of power, strength, and honor became a position of weakness, neediness, shame, and insecurity. She lost her source, the Father. She was physically separated from His Spirit, which surrounded her, and her empty, aching heart now longs for man to fill the void. This is the new flow for the encompasser. This is her new life.

Man was also affected by woman's new flow. Man and woman were created to flow in tandem—to act and react, to ebb and flow all within the Spirit of God, the energy of life. The life God breathed into them was to flow through and between them, back and forth. We react/respond because we were made to do so, to flow in harmony and unity and power. Because of the Fall, however, woman began to crave man, and he, in response, began to flow sin and death back to her. Man's intention became to rule over woman rather than to protect her. Just as she no longer flows toward him with life, he no longer responds by flowing back to her with life. He has become the stifling, oppressive container; his new response is ruling over her need, pushing her and her need away, controlling her, repressing her and subduing her.

This corruption to their design is the start of disunity between the sexes and is the reason for the power struggle between men and women. In the male/female relationship, there is POWER. Their original design was a power couple! There would be no power *struggle* if there wasn't any power. This power can be recaptured. We can return to who we were before the Fall, when woman functioned as man's the perfect design of the Father and not the corrupt design. We can return to a place of unity with each other and with the Lord. We can once again rule over the planet and function as one flesh and be blessed.

TIME FOR A NEW NAME

Women are one key to this restoration. We can grab onto the hope that He is extending to us. We can have our relationships filled once again with peace and unity and power. I think one of the best parts of the story of the Fall is the hope it contains. When the consequences of man's and woman's actions are explained— as they grieve their losses and receive in their very bodies the consequences of their choices—it is at that very moment that the man decides to name the woman. In that name, there is hope. If you remember, when man and woman were created, they functioned with one shared name: adam, or "mankind." However, death and corruption came to their relationship and caused separation between them. This separation was so drastic that it caused woman to need her own name. She would no longer share the name "Adam." When a new name is given in the Bible, we know that something significant took place or is about to take place in or through that person. "Abram" to "Abraham," "Sarai" to "Sarah," "Jacob" to "Israel," and "Saul" to "Paul" are all examples of new names given at significant times. Names explain and symbolize the person, their calling, or a change in them.

THE FALL OF MANKIND

In the midst of corruption and separation, woman gets a new name, and that name tells us more about her design.

Genesis 3:19–21 says, "For from dust you were made and to dust you shall return. *Now the man called his wife's name Eve because she was the source of life.* And the Lord made clothing of skin for them and He clothed them" (NIV, emphasis added).

In this moment, in the midst of loss, it is not the Father but Adam who decides that a new name is needed. God had named woman "Adam" or "Mankind" because she was and is an equal part of mankind. Adam had named her "Woman" (meaning taken from man, and this also means wife) when she was taken from him. Now, when woman was further separated from him, Adam decided she needed another new name.

Although the Fall was a sad moment in which mankind was given a new picture of death and loss, there was also hope, as it is with God who always provides a way out for us. In Adam's choice of name, I hear that hope. He could have named her anything. Let's not forget that Adam and Eve had just heard the pronouncement that they had lost everything, and just before that, Adam blamed Eve completely. In that moment, with this mindset, he could have named her something negative and awful, something like "The Giver of Death" or "Thanks to You, We Lost Everything." However, Adam must have had a change of heart. He must have taken those few moments to allow God to touch him and comfort him, as God does when His children are hurting. Then Adam stepped out as the leader he was created to be and gave her a beautiful, hope-filled name: "Eve." In *Strong's Concordance*, "eve" is H2332 *chavvah*, which simply translates as "life," or "life-giving." It can also be translated as "source of life." Adam was declaring, "I have named her Life Giver because she is the source of life, and every time I say her name, I will remember who she is and will remember what her place is with me and with mankind."

He could more clearly see her identity, and he didn't want either of them to forget it. He understood that woman is the source of life. She was designed to bring life, and Adam understood that more clearly now because she had brought death. He was supposed to watch out for her and protect her because she is the source of life. She is the encompasser, the one who flows around them, and she is the one who was designed to surround them with life.

Also, in his naming, I hear Adam speaking prophetically over womankind. He bestowed upon her a name that would remind them both of better days to come. He was forgiving her, encouraging her, comforting her, and releasing hope. Every time Adam said her new name, he and she would remember that she was meant to flow life and to circle around them with the life energy of God's Spirit. Woman was created as the female expression of God, the part of mankind that nurtures life. She is Woman. She is Adam. She is the e*zer kennegdo* and the encompasser. She is Eve.

Popular church teachings say Eve got her name because she was the mother of humankind. I do believe that being a life-giving mother is part of who Eve was. Part of God's command to Adam and Eve was to multiply, and Eve did become the mother of all humankind. "Mother" was certainly a part of her identity. Yet, a new name marks something significant and new. Naming Eve "Mother" at this moment—as some new and novel idea—just doesn't make sense. Eve was already going to be the mother of all; this wasn't something new. Her motherhood had already been established in their call and when the Lord separated them into two bodies so they could multiply. If the name "Eve" only meant "mother," why didn't she receive it then? She didn't because the real power in her name was so much bigger than just being a mother. She was designed to encompass with the power of life. She would reproduce and pour out life energy upon this planet. *This* is the reason she received a new name. *God* named her "mankind," and *man* named her "life giver." This is who women are.

Women are an important part of mankind. We were designed to carry the heart of the Lord to this planet. We are the source of life in many ways: we birth children, we nurture, we care. We have hearts that birth ideas, businesses, and ministries. That is our design and our name. We give life to our children, and we can bring life energy to our families and to our men. Our influence is critical on this hurting planet. Men need us and the children of the world need us. The Lord is ready to heal, reconcile, restore, and bring us back to our position of power and value. In the next chapter we will look at where women are today and at how our "intense craving" plays out in generation after generation. Let us hold onto the hope that He is ready with the answer. We are the source of life, and we will be restored to the fullness of it.

CAN WE TAKE A MOMENT TO PRAY?

Let us together, as women, thank the Lord for who He has made us and how He has made us.

Father, we thank You. Thank You for making us women. Thank You for giving us the ability to carry Your heart to this planet. Thank You for designing us that we would be close to You, that we would be close to Your Spirit, that we would carry Your life-giving Presence to the world. Thank You for making us life givers and the source of life. Thank You that we can birth and nurture and raise children and bring life to them. Thank You that we are able to supply life to our men, to our sons and brothers and all the men in our world. Thank You, especially, that we have the pleasure and the privilege to supply life and love and influence to our husbands, that we can bring to them what they need. Thank You, Father, and please help us to walk and talk, every day, as the women You designed us to be. We love You and we thank You for loving us.

4

THE CORRUPT PATTERN: WOMEN INTENSELY CRAVE AND MEN RULE OVER

"She put on her earrings and jewels and went out to look for her lovers but forgot all about Me, says the Lord."
‖ Hosea 2:13

"We are all cracked; that's how the light gets in."
‖ "Anthem" by Leonard Cohen[32]

We ended our last chapter with Adam and Eve leaving the Garden, their home, as orphans. Their sin released death to them and all the planet. They lost everything. Their powerful dynamic as "encompasser and container," their original perfect design, was corrupted. Eve could no longer function according to her original design as the *ezer kennegdo* with the power and strength of God; that position was corrupted. She could no longer encompass Adam with the Spirit of God and life, because death touched her and set new death-filled consequences in motion. Within this corrupted design, Eve began to intensely crave Adam, and he began to rule over her.

Eve was filled with grief, and along with everything else, she also lost her Father. She could not run to Him with her orphaned heart full of pain. She could not run to Him for comfort nor sit in His presence for peace. She was alone with her pain. This inner ache is what fueled her new corrupted position of craving and need. Her design was still the same: she would still encompass Adam, and he would still respond back to her. Except, instead of encompassing him with life and God's Spirit, she would now encompass him with her need, fueled by her pain, as she sought her own relief. Man became her source and the answer to her ache. God has been replaced in her life.

The narrative in Genesis is a factual recording of mankind's history, and it reads in a factual way, without mention of Adam's and Eve's emotional states. It is easy to read this passage of scripture and miss the emotion of this moment. However, if we take a moment to think on it, we can begin to understand what Adam and Eve were feeling. Consider one of your own experiences of loss and compare it to theirs. Imagine a time of grief you experienced, and then think about what they experienced. They lost everything in one moment. Everything they had and everything they were a part of died. They had never experienced death before it touched every part of them—including their relationships and their planet. Even more painful was the fact that it was their own fault. On top of the pain of their loss was the pain of their regret. They could not turn to the Father for comfort because they had lost their connection with Him. They could take no comfort in their home because their beautiful garden, in which they had been surrounded by the Holy Spirit and by life, was gone too. They grieved the death they had released to the planet and had no place of comfort.

Death brought corruption, and corruption touched the entire planet. The Bible says in Isaiah 25:7 that death actually is like a veil or a canopy that is stretched over the entire planet. Romans 8:20–23 reminds us that all of creation is under bondage to corruption and is groaning for liberation. It groans because it is covered with a veil of death energy. All people are born under this death and need to be saved from its effects. Every baby that

THE CORRUPT PATTERN:
WOMEN INTENSELY CRAVE AND MEN RULE OVER

is born comes into the world under the canopy or veil of death on a planet in desperate need of restoration. This is where the idea of mankind's burden of original sin comes from—that we all inherited this death and corruption. The death and corruption that Eve encompassed and Adam released continue to hold the planet and all people under its power.

First Corinthians 15:22 says that we all die because we all came from Adam. Romans 5:12–14,17 says it best: "When Adam sinned, sin entered the entire human race. His sin spread death throughout all the world, so everything began to grow old and die, for all sinned. We know that it was Adam's sin that caused this because although, of course, people were sinning from the time of Adam until Moses, God did not in those days judge them guilty of death for breaking his laws—because He had not yet given His laws to them nor told them what He wanted them to do. *So when their bodies died it was not for their own sins since they themselves had never disobeyed God's special law against eating the forbidden fruit, as Adam had*...For this one man, Adam, brought death to many through *his sin*...*The sin of this one man, Adam*, caused death to be king over all" (TLB, emphasis added). This is what all of mankind inherited from Adam and Eve. Unfortunately, Adam and Eve did not reproduce from their original design but from their corrupted one. This death is what they reproduced. Death was around them as well as in them, as it is in every person born after them.

As Dr. Francis Myles states in his powerful book *The Order of Melchizedek,* "Since the fall of Adam and Eve, men and women have been ravaged by sin and its dreadful power. When sin entered the world, it unleashed death agencies into the spiritual atmosphere of the fallen Adamic kingdom we now call our world. These death agencies released by sin also corrupted the human gene pool, making every child born of a woman a prisoner of sin from their first breathing moment outside the womb."[33]

Each person on this planet was born into this corruption. Every child *is* born as a prisoner of sin and as an abandoned, rejected "orphan." The loss of our Father at the Fall caused all mankind to be born without the Father; we are all orphans at birth. The Bible specifically calls the *fatherless* orphans, and that is what Adam and Eve became and what we are now, until the day that we accept and appropriate what we are given from Christ's sacrificial death on a cross.

Each little girl is born into the corrupted relationship dynamic Eve began when she and Adam ate the fruit, and every person is born into the position of orphan. When Adam and Eve lost the purity of their relationship and their position with the Father, so did everyone who followed in their genetic line. We reproduce what we are. Our original parents were orphans, so we are born as orphans too. Our orphaned heart is in pain, and we, as Eve, seek relief. We all seek relief from our pain and emptiness in something. This pain is what fuels woman's "intense craving" for a man. Eve's heart was full of pain and emptiness, and her offspring followed in this pattern. Women are born with this longing, or maybe better said, we are born into it. We are born into a corrupt desire for a man and into an empty orphan's heart. Until Jesus came to seek and save that which was lost, until He provided redemption, until His sacrifice on the cross and victory over death, there was no solution. To some degree, this corrupted dynamic has been repeated over and over, in every woman, every man, and in every relationship.

I believe that most men and women function today from this pattern of the corrupted dynamics, which were created at the Fall and which have been passed down through the generations. We continue to live from this place of compromised design and corrupted dynamics and not from who we were originally created to be. Instead of the perfect flow of the Holy Spirit from male to female, we live here, in a pattern created by death released at the

THE CORRUPT PATTERN:
WOMEN INTENSELY CRAVE AND MEN RULE OVER

Fall. We are in bondage to this corruption—until we are saved from it. Romans 8:20–23 says, "The creation itself also will be set free *from its slavery to corruption* into the freedom of the glory of the children of God. For we know that the *whole* creation groans and suffers... together until now" (NIV, emphasis added). Everything came into bondage to corruption. The entire planet and all it contains—all people, animals, plants, everything—are subject to corruption until they are set free. Man, woman, and their relationship are under this same bondage until they are restored.

Everyone to some degree or another carries this needy, orphaned heart. For those of you who have been hurt, your heart is filled with even deeper wounds and unmet emotional needs Many of you were abused, some even as babies. The awareness of being unwanted, abandoned, and rejected is felt both consciously and also buried deep in your subconscious. However, even those of you who were blessed with loving parents—parents who wanted you, who welcomed you into the world with joy and acceptance, parents who cared for you—even you were born with the heart of an orphan, and at some level you carry that pain. Not only do we all carry some degree of the pain of our orphan state but also even the healthiest person has unmet emotional needs. We all have needs. Women need to feel safe and secure. Most women need to know that they are beautiful and desired. Most women need to know that they are cared for and protected. All women need to know that they are loved. The bigger problem for us comes when we don't take our needs or wounds to God. Whether our pain is on the surface or has been buried under many years of abuse or denial, only God can completely heal our hearts from all pain and all of our wounds, and only He can completely meet our needs for love and acceptance.

Unfortunately, because we have inherited the corrupted pattern of intense craving for a man, women automatically turn to men with our orphaned hearts and our unmet needs that cry out for relief.

Over and over we see women living from this corrupted relationship pattern. I have worked in women's ministry for many years, and I've seen and heard the struggles of women of all ages, and I know my own struggles as well. It is clear, women certainly do crave after men. There are single women who do not feel complete without a man and think that a man will solve all their problems; they live emotionally stuck lives waiting for their knight in shining armor to show up. There are women who chase after a man, desperate or even manipulative and doing whatever they can to get just crumbs of attention. There are women who give up their bodies, their self-esteem, their money, and even their children for even a fleeting moment of affection or provision. There are women who stay in abusive or unhealthy relationships because they think they need a man; they fear being without him and alone; they fear not being able to take care of themselves financially. There are women who spend their time and energy trying to demand change or to manipulate their men to change. There are married women who take their inner ache to their husband to fill, falsely thinking that they would feel better if they could get their husband to do more or be more: to leave work at a decent time, get out of the garage, and get away from the TV. From their "craving" they are hoping their knight in shining armor will change and charge in on his white horse and make everything better. I hear many married women say things like, "If my husband would do X, our problems would be solved" or "If my husband would do Y, our lives would be better" or "If he loved me, if he would pick up his socks, remember my birthday, be more loving to our kids, notice my haircut, spend more time with the family, work less, or work more..." and on and on. This is Eve's consequence, that we inherited, working through us. *Getting* a man or *fixing* our current man is *not* the answer to the ache of our unmet needs and the deep cries of our heart.

I have lived out of this corrupted dynamic and have seen many other women live it too. I have had more than one husband and, when I was younger, boyfriend after boyfriend. I have looked for love in all the wrong places. I have desired to be cherished by someone, only to find that I had once again married or connected with someone who was either unable or unwilling to love me (at least this is how I explained it to myself). Then off I would go again, in search of another man to love me. I was completely controlled by the "intense craving" that I inherited from Eve. Although God has been healing me all along the way, I have had many broken relationships and have spent many nights crying myself to sleep. The most powerful healing came as God took me through the revelations in this book. Step by step, He had me walk out these truths as He revealed them to me deep in my spirit. Ladies, from the depth of my heart, I understand the struggle and the pain of the corrupted design.

WE MAKE MEN OUR IDOLS

What the Lord has shown me is that the intense craving for a man is really idolatry, as we see in the book of Hosea and our foundational Jeremiah 31:22 scripture, which begins with "How long will you go here and there, o faithless daughter..." What we inherited from Eve and the women before us is an idolatrous relationship with men. "Idolatry" is an old-fashioned word, but it is the best word to explain this relationship dynamic. "Idolatry" is the worship of or devotion to anything that you have chosen *in place of God* to be your God. What are we to look to God for? Peace, love, security, protection, answers, hope, help, direction, provision, all and everything we could ever need. We are to look to God to help us, to guide us, to provide for us, to heal us, to defend us, to protect us, to define us and basically everything we need. When Eve lost her connection with God, she had to find a replacement. God told her that her corrupted position would cause her to look to Adam instead of Him. Basically, women are born into a relationship where we choose men in place of God; we look to men to be our God. Many women now look to men for provision, security, love, and all the things we are to look to God for. We take to them our list. Provide for me, make me feel safe, help me, give me, love me, and on and on we go.

Idolatry also includes the concept of worship or devotion. We worship what we idolize. We are devoted. We make sacrifices for them. We have within us the inherent craving and desire after a man, an idolatrous relationship with man, and so we will worship and sacrifice to him. I know that I have sacrificed many things just to make or keep a relationship with a man. I'm sure many of you have too. Maybe you spend money on your appearance. Maybe you spend your time and energy thinking about him, wondering if he's going to call, wondering if he's thinking about you. Maybe you deny your feelings or needs and compromise your true self to keep the peace and to keep from upsetting or losing him. But when you stay in an unhappy or unhealthy relationship, you sacrifice your own health. You may even sacrifice your children. Ultimately, when you idolize a man, you sacrifice yourself.

Women repeat this pattern of looking to a man to be our everything over and over. Do we even stop and question ourselves? It seems that we do not; it has become an unconscious part of who we are as women. We all know women whose entire lives are structured around this need for a man. We all know women who lose weight, get plastic surgery, and even expose too much of their body and dress suggestively—all for a man's pleasure. We know women who allow their personal lives or professional lives to be subjected to this need for a man. They work two jobs because he refuses to work or to improve himself professionally. We all know women who have made choices about their education, their profession, or their business based on how it would affect a man they had or a man they wanted. Many times we structure our entire day, week, or life around men. Of course, there are times within healthy relationships where we compromise, and we *do* make sacrifices for the family or our marriage. That is inevitable and a necessary part of family life. What I am referring to here is when it is unhealthy, out of balance, when our motives are from a heart that is wanting to please, pacify, or attract a man so that we feel loved or needed or special or, at the very least, so that we are not abandoned by him.

Also, worth saying here, it is true that some of you have stable marriages and feel fulfilled and don't feel as if this applies to your life. If that is you, I applaud you and thank God for you! I know some women who function with their husbands in a very powerful one-flesh relationship; although unaware of this dynamic, they have lived it. These are the rare women who may have had relatively happy childhoods filled with love and security and who do have deep, meaningful relationships with God that are full of health and maturity. If that is you, reading this book will help you understand how and why you have been freed to live so well and give you insight into how you can help other women. However, I also know women who have stable and happy marriages yet who never let God deep down inside their hearts. They have been loved and cared for, but they have filled themselves with their husbands in places that belong to God. Maybe their husbands are loving and attentive and are eager to pour love into their wives, and that deep inner ache was partially filled but the real depth has never been addressed or healed. I would challenge you to ask God to show you if that is you. Ask Him to help you to give Him full access to your heart, to make *Him* your Husband *first*. He is faithful to show you what you need. I trust Him to make your marriage even better than it already is.

I am confident to say that in all my years of experience, I have found that most of us women live with this intense craving for a man. If you can, picture this craving on a continuum of behavior. On one end is accepting the intense craving for a man and operating from that craving, and at the other end is rejecting and denying that craving. There are many points along the way. You could move along this continuum from year to year and from relationship to relationship. At the far end of the spectrum is a rejection of the craving; there are women who deny it and who choose to live without "needing" men nor letting men have a significant influence in their lives. Their internal craving for a man has instead become an angry refusal of that craving; it is a denial of the desire we have been born into. Sometimes they become men haters or men bashers and can become angry and bitter. Sometimes they become "superwomen" who overfunction, outdo and outperform the men in their lives. This is just as dangerous as being on the other end of the continuum. The Lord created men and women to function in tandem, to reflect His image of a united Trinity. He intended for us to need each other in a healthy, positive way. The original design was for us to function together, complement each other, and walk in power and unity. When we reject men or cut them out of our lives, we reject the design of God. This is, in a sense, spiritual lesbianism, which keeps us diminished from who we could be. It is just as unhealthy as the other end of the continuum of women who live consumed with their "intense craving" for a man. Wherever you are on this spectrum or continuum is irrelevant; you are still functioning from your inherited position and you will be on this continuum, living in some response to this "craving," until it is healed.

THE CORRUPT PATTERN:
WOMEN INTENSELY CRAVE AND MEN RULE OVER

Whether we are chasing men or rejecting them, seducing them or insulting them, seeing them as our saviors or regarding them as our rivals, the consequences that Eve received are alive and well in women. The women who reject men are doing the same thing as the women who chase men: they are acting from or reacting to the "intense craving" that they spiritually inherited. At either end of this spectrum are women who want to capture, manipulate, or eliminate the heart of men (and their craving for it) in order to feel safe, loved, or complete. If you examine yourself, many of you will see that you are somewhere on this continuum, too. Again, for some of you, God has healed parts of your heart without you realizing what was being healed, but now you can understand more fully. Wherever you are, or wherever you have been, you have had to settle this issue. It is the same for every woman in every culture. *It is the cry of the orphan that fuels the corrupted position we were born into, and the only solution is God.* Until God heals us, every woman to some degree or another lives under this corrupt dynamic. It is pervasive and a deep part of who we are—so deep that it has actually become a subconscious bondage for many of us. When we are healed from this intense craving, we can return to our powerful original design and can fully and correctly relate with men. But until we are healed from it, we are bound to it.

Many factors work together to keep women bound to this corrupted pattern we inherited. Yes, we are born into it; however, the bondage is strengthened by many other things. We have inherited generational beliefs and patterns from those who came before us that solidify this corrupted design. We received the conscious or subconscious messages of our mothers and grandmothers as they lived out their "intense craving" before our eyes. In addition, culture also works to strengthen our corrupt pattern. Culture draws us toward the corrupted male/female dynamic through books, movies, songs, and other storylines. Politics, governments, and other cultural institutions underscore the corrupt pattern of men and women. We have an Enemy who knows the power of our original design, and he does everything he can to keep us away from it and bound to the corrupted design. The Enemy works through these things to create deeper and deeper strongholds. However, our own lack of understanding and the errors that we have accepted about who we are and what we were designed to be are what make us vulnerable to the lies of the Enemy, and the powerful influence of all these factors together strengthens our bondage to this corrupt pattern.

GENERATIONAL INFLUENCE

Think about your own childhood. What messages about men were directly or indirectly spoken? Maybe you heard messages that said that having a man is the answer. That a man will fix everything. That if you're single, you need to get a man. Or maybe you heard messages from the other end of the continuum: never trust a man, learn how to take care of yourself, women are better than men. As children, we believe what we're told. We are impressed at early ages with thoughts and beliefs that stay with us. Examine your heart. Think about the messages you may have received. Did you have a mother, grandmother, aunt, or big sister who modeled the corrupt dynamic? What messages about gender and gender roles or power and powerlessness did you learn? We pass along beliefs that strengthen women's intense craving for a man throughout the generations, and we pass on pain and emotional issues too. In some families, generation after generation struggles with the pain of addictions, or incest, or divorce, or a myriad of other dysfunctions. These wounds only intensify the deep ache to be loved, to be safe and protected, and to be cared for.

We can't blame our parents or grandparents; they too were living out this corrupted pattern to some degree. Our mothers may have not had any understanding of or ability to live in God's Spirit, and they could only give what they received from the generations before them. What we received strengthens and fortifies the corrupt dynamic we all received from Eve. What we received from previous generations solidifies the power of our corrupted position. They modeled it, and we followed. They gave us the messages, and we believed. They didn't know the truth about who men and women really are, so they could teach us nothing but the error that they had received. In our ignorance, because we don't know better, we continue to perpetuate women who either intensely crave men or reject them.

THE PULL OF CULTURE

The powerful pull of culture solidifies the corrupt dynamic every day. Just look at Instagram or Facebook or any social media site, and you will see women reacting to men from one end of the spectrum to the other. The theme of women either intensely craving men or rejecting them is in the stories and songs and sayings of our time. We have read about the woman who sought a man, eventually captured him, and then lived happily ever after. But we have also heard the voices of women who have rejected that craving and have insulted men instead. We see this in culture too: women band together with political ideologies and agendas that are based on their refusal and denial of their intense craving for a man. Often we see family television programs that portray the husband/father as a bumbling fool, with kids who ridicule him! The corrupted position of women is being lived out in our culture, day after day.

Look at the plot line for most of Disney's princesses: A young, beautiful woman is struggling through some sort of pain, problem, difficulty, or need. A prince comes to fight for her and solves every problem. The princess's heart and life are filled with love, and she lives happily ever after. What a powerful way to fill the deep pain of the orphaned heart; this type of story encourages girls to envision a future in which they intensely crave a man. A little girl is left to either accept this idea, reject it, or bounce back and forth as she works to decide. These are the fairy tales that girls hear and the movies that they watch: stories about women who need men. Even stories with powerful women often involve a man who rescues them and romances them in some way. This is how we grow up to become women who ache to be wanted, desired, loved, and cherished by a man. We want to be pursued by our knight on his white horse. These aches to be loved, cherished and pursued are not the *problem*; they are a part of womanhood. The problem comes when we take these desires to a *man* and expect him to fill us. If we first take these aches and desires to God, let Him fill them, and then we can better relate to men. However, most of us just want a *man* to come and fight for us and rescue us. Facing the absence of such a man, we might completely reject our ache and refuse to acknowledge it. Either way, the corrupted position of Eve is being handed to our girls.

You know what concept isn't popular in our culture? The one that says that women are powerful and satisfied in and by our God. The one that explains that women have an important position on Earth as the source of life and as men's perfect, opposite counterpart. We do not see that explained, modeled or taught. We are not taught that women are a valuable part of mankind and that we carry the feminine expression of God to this world. We are not taught that God is enough for us and that we can be filled with all we need from Him. We are not taught to encompass our world and our men with all God has put inside us. We are not honored or valued for what we bring to men. Our voices are not celebrated or even sought after. Our original design is not part of our culture. It isn't in most of the messages we receive, nor is it generally modeled by our female mentors.

DEMONIC PRESSURE

There is a Devil, and he and his demons are well aware of our corrupted position. They know how ineffective we are when we function within our broken design, and they know the pain it causes us. The Devil was present with mankind when they *all* heard how death had corrupted them. He heard the consequences they would experience for releasing death unto the planet. The Devil knows our original design; he used it against us to destroy us. He knew that we were created to be powerful, to work together as one flesh, and to use our authority over the planet to rule as God's representatives. The Enemy knows our corrupted design and how to work it against us. He knows all of this, and he knows he must keep us in the dark and away from the truth that will set us free. He enjoys the pain this causes. He came to steal, kill, and destroy, and that is clearly what happens in our relationships with the opposite sex. He stole our unity, our authority, our identity, and our position as one flesh, and he keeps us from regaining our original power.

For years, our corrupted position has been a tool in the hand of the Enemy. He works our corrupted design against us. He encourages women to intensely crave men, and as he knows, our needs can never be fully met by men, and we will be left unfulfilled and hurt. *Even the best husband makes for a very poor God.* They cannot fill the depth of our need, and the enemy knows that. He wants us to keep yearning and reaching for what we will never fully have: a man to fill our heart completely. He also knows man's response to us, and he encourages men to push us away, oppress us, and abandon us. This causes our craving to intensify, or it causes us to spiral into denial and rejection. Around we go in this cycle, pushed along by the Enemy. He spins us like a top and lets us go around and around the cycle of our corrupted dynamic in motion, strengthening patterns that we are bound to repeat. The Enemy uses whatever he can to keep us spinning; he uses culture, generational sin, and even our own ignorance of our true selves. This is repeated every day and in every culture.

Can you imagine what the world would be like if most of us were able to function from our original design? If we could walk in unity and without conflict? If man and woman could receive the best from each other? If women would receive and respect men as the containers/protectors/leaders of mankind? If men would value and accept women to be the powerful life-givers and encompassers of mankind? If men would listen to our voices and cherish and value what we give them? If men would contain and protect us and not rule over or exploit us? That would be power on Earth, because we would be functioning in God's image, releasing the Father and establishing His kingdom. There is no way the Enemy wants that. He works hard to keep us fighting, to keep us separated, to keep us believing the lies about who we are and about who we are to each other. He knows the pain that women endure by the hand of men. We are "ruled over"; we are abused and oppressed and rejected. The Enemy enjoys hurting women as he stirs men to oppress them or abandon them. He keeps us hurting as much as he can. The Devil hates women because he knows his fate; one day we will rise up and crush his head (see Genesis 3:15). I believe that day has come.

THE CORRUPT PATTERN:
WOMEN INTENSELY CRAVE AND MEN RULE OVER

MEN RESPOND WITH RULING OVER

Eve was told she would have an intense craving for man, and since she was created to function in tandem with man, he would *respond* to this craving. He would respond by "ruling over" her. Allow me to loosely paraphrase the Lord's message to woman in Genesis 3 to something like: "Because you set the tone and create the flow in your relationship, the man's position is affected by you. He was designed to respond to you. Your position is corrupted, and now you will surround him with your need. He will react and respond to you differently than he was designed to. I am not changing the original design, however. You were built to function in tandem, as one, and you will continue to function in tandem, except it is not with My Spirit." Yes, we do function in tandem; as we desire after them, they respond. Man's original response was to *contain* woman, protect her, and lead her, but his position was corrupted. He was to contain her by carrying her and holding her inside himself. However, the word "contain" has other meanings. It can also mean to restrain, suppress, and oppress. In his corrupted container position, man restrains and oppresses her and suppresses her need.

Bernadette Mosala once said, "When men are oppressed, it's tragedy. When women are oppressed, it's tradition."

We see this across generations and in every culture: men oppressing women. Do we not have countless examples of horrific oppressions that women have lived under for centuries. Entire societies have been built around the consequences of the Fall; in these societies, males dominate and women are oppressed. Even in more "evolved" societies, we still see men "ruling over" women and we see this all over the world. They oppress them, rape them, abuse them, objectify them, own them, and profit from them. The entire sex industry is based on men who use, objectify, dominate, and profit from women as they exploit them. The "ruling over" spirit is clearly seen in the exploitation of women. Sex slavery and the buying and selling of women occurs in every country and culture. There are millions of women or girls who have gone missing and who are assumed to be victims of trafficking, which is an industry mainly operated by men. Whether they are the ones selling or buying, these men are acting from the "ruling over women" spirit. Many men blatantly oppress women through intimidation, pornography, violence, and all sorts of other abuses. Men oppress women politically, economically, and emotionally. This "ruling over" spirit is seen in the attitudes and behaviors that silence women's voices. Sexist jokes and sexist remarks dishonor or insult women. Even seemingly innocent remarks can diminish women and strengthen conflict. Sometimes "ruling over" comes in other forms; it can even be the religious voices that say "women cannot lead" or "women must not preach in church" or the errors in applying the concept of submission. Unfortunately, we are oftentimes told that submission is the silent acceptance of whatever a man does, which often fuels the "ruling over" spirit. This concept of submission based on the corrupted design of Adam and Eve looks very different than the concept of submission based on the original design of unity, oneness, and equal power. Women in the church have had too much teaching from a slanted perspective of what "submission" means. I find many women resentful about this concept, but if women understood the design of God, then submission to their man and honor to all men could be given willingly and from the heart. There will be more on that later, but for now, I wanted to be sure to point out that "ruling over" can come draped in religious clothing and is not always easy to see.

THE CORRUPT PATTERN:
WOMEN INTENSELY CRAVE AND MEN RULE OVER

"Ruling over" is also a continuum of behavior, and men can function from either end of the spectrum. One end is oppression and the other end is abandonment. One end is abuse of power and the opposite end of the same continuum of "ruling over" is men who have left their place and who choose to hide. Either way, men *respond* to our need of and intense craving for them. We have looked a bit at men who oppress, so let's look at the other end of the continuum. Men on the abandoning end of the spectrum are men who may fear women and their intense needs. They fear that they are not enough to contain us or meet our needs. They fear that they cannot handle us, and so they hide. Also, some men may have had examples from abusive fathers who hurt their mothers, and they don't want to be that man; they don't want to abuse or oppress so they may instead choose the abandonment end of the spectrum. But until they are freed, they too are bound to the corrupt pattern. They were designed to *respond* to us. They were designed to function with us as one and in tandem. If we demand that they meet our needs, if we chase them, looking for them to solve our inner ache, *they must respond*; that's the design. Whatever we encompass them with requires a response from them. If they are not going to oppress, and push us and our need down, then they may run away, hide from us, reject us, and abandon us. They may even attempt to meet our needs, bending over backward, jumping through any hoop, trying to give us whatever will make us happy, which eventually ends with resentment and exhaustion. In any case, they are responding to us. At the far end of the continuum are the men who disconnect in any way they can. This could look like single men who refuse to commit to a woman or marry; they hide their hearts from women yet they might use or exploit them. This could be married men who hide their hearts too; they hide from their wives, their children, and their place in the home. They hide in the garage or in their work or in some addiction that will keep them disconnected. Maybe they run to pornography and hide themselves and their sexuality in something that doesn't need them and can't reject them. Or perhaps they leave their wives and their families through divorce. They abandon women emotionally, physically, spiritually, and financially. Sometimes men hide because they have been betrayed or beaten down by women who were overly critical, judgmental, and demanding of them. Many men have broken hearts from women who, in their intense craving, jump from man to man, manipulating them, playing games, and seeking only their own relief. In their quest to be loved, some women hurt men and push them toward hiding their hearts. The end result is the same: women who are left with pain and emptiness and men who function from the "ruling over" spirit.

WHEN MEN RULE AND WOMEN CRAVE

The corrupted relationship dynamic is really the modern day's power struggle between men and women. Women, we start the flow. We were designed to keep the relationship flowing from our internal position. Remember, we created a circuit of energy that flowed around men and our relationships. We were designed to create this flow, this atmosphere, and to encircle them to strengthen our oneness and unity with them. Yet, under the corrupted dynamic, this flow creates conflict. We encompass men with our flow of intense need for them to make us feel better, fill us, and love us, and they respond back, as they were created to. We send an energy that demands and craves and needs. They respond to that by either pushing it away, pushing it down, running away, or something similar. If we come from the other end of the continuum and send to them an energy that rejects them, they again respond back by overpowering us or withdrawing further. Either way, the woman is only strengthened to reject them even more. Disunity and conflict increase, and the dynamic deepens and continues.

From whatever place they hold on the continuum, women surround men with their "internal flow," their influence, and men respond back as they were created to do. But men and women relating to each other from anywhere on these two behavior continuums will end up in conflict. There is no unity or oneness in these positions; there is only more hurt, more pain, more conflict and a strengthening to the gap that separates and divides us. Yes, men and women are different. But we are also one another's perfect counterpoints, equal in power; both our positions are valuable and important and are made to perfectly complement each other. We were made to function in unity. Should we accept that there is a power struggle? Can we just accept that there is power in the relationship between men and women and that we can restore the power and remove the struggle? I believe that we can when we function from our original design. However, when we live from our corrupted design and dynamic, we only create more conflict and heartache.

WHEN WE COME TOGETHER, WE CAN BE THE TRINITY ON EARTH

In Genesis, God created mankind in His image with His purpose. Men and women were to function as one entity: one person, two bodies, fulfilling a joint call. They were to rule with unbroken fellowship and would be blessed with extravagant gifts. They were to be blessed, united, and powerful. Can you picture our society if men and women functioned this way today? Can you imagine the love, honor, and respect that would grow between them? For years, we've had a power struggle between the sexes, but what if the struggle was gone? Then there would only be power, just as when God originally created the first power couple, mankind. The truth is, *all* couples were designed to be power couples.

We have been far away from God's perfect design for a long time. His beautiful, precious women are hurting. His precious daughters are exposing themselves, degrading themselves, pouring out their lives and finances, and allowing themselves to be used, abused, and overlooked. This tears at the heart of our Father. He aches for His women who are angry and hurt because of the men who oppress them. He hurts for His women who have rejected men and, in doing so, have rejected a part of themselves. He hears the single women who cry out in their loneliness, asking for a man. He hears the cries of married women who plead with Him, "Change my husband. He is hurting me so badly." He knows that many women have just given up and stopped caring or hoping for more. His desire is to return us all back to our original design. He wants to heal. He wants to heal you. And for every woman who already has a measure of strength and wholeness in this area, He wants to give you more, and He wants to give you clarity so you can help other women be free, too. His heart is with us, ladies. And His heart is with the men too. He didn't create them to dominate us nor did He create them to be passive and weak; He created them to contain, lead, and protect us. He wants to restore that. I feel it every day. I hear Him and His heart for His people.

I would like to end this chapter with a journal entry from my own life, from years ago. I have many years of experience of living out the corrupted position we all inherited from Eve; I have suffered all the pain of orphan DNA. Some years, all I wanted was a man to make the pain go away. I went through boyfriend after boyfriend, then husband after husband. I also had times in my life when I said, "Forget it. I don't need a man," and I functioned too independently with my heart full of hurt and anger. I've done it all. This journal entry is from a time in my life when my husband and I were rapidly approaching divorce, and the Lord was using that time to help me understand more of this revelation. It seems fitting to add this excerpt to this chapter.

THE CORRUPT PATTERN:
WOMEN INTENSELY CRAVE AND MEN RULE OVER

MY JOURNAL ENTRY

"Lord, I just want to be loved. I want to know I am worth it. And beautiful. I need his attention. I can feel my heart actually ache.

Day after day he ignores me. He doesn't even give me eye contact. We exist in the same space as total strangers. It literally feels like I am dying every day. I am crying as I write this knowing how deeply I am affected. How deep is my desire to be loved? What is wrong with me???

I walk around feeling so ugly and fat and old. I can barely tolerate looking at my reflection. I look in the mirror and want to cry at what I see. An old, ugly woman is what I see, and I guess he sees it too. He is probably as repulsed by me as I am. I wish he understood how desperately I need him to touch me, which he never does...to tell me I am beautiful, to act like he is attracted to me. It never happens.

I want to share my heart with him, but he doesn't want it. I try to talk to him, but he isn't listening. He clearly is not interested in me sharing my heart or in anything I have to say. I talk and he glazes over or looks away at his phone or his watch. He never asks how my day was or how I am. He knows nothing about me, and I can't share with him anything that is important to me. I can't tell him when I am excited about something wonderful because he will probably say something negative or he just won't care or maybe not even listen. I can't tell him if I am having any problems with anything because he will find a way to tell me it is my fault. He will blame me and criticize me and not care about how I feel. My heart is not safe with him. Lord, You see what is happening!!!!!

I am lying in bed another night and crying because I am so lonely. I cry because I am left every night with an empty marriage and a broken heart. I can't keep doing this! I am too old to keep living this way, and what about my kids? This is not the way I want them to live! Please help them to do better than I am. Heal my girls that they pick good men who will cherish them.

You are all I have. But who do I really need more than You?

I take my heart to him over and over and open my heart to him only to be left empty, to be rejected again, to be hurt and ignored and abused. Then I walk away crying to You. This is our pattern. Why?? This is sick and crazy, and I am done. I am done with this. Why don't I just sit with You? I need to cry at Your feet that You would make me feel beautiful to You. I can tell You all the things in my heart that I would try and tell him. Why don't I let You love on me that way? Why???

I feel unlovable. I hate this.

There is something about me that is unlovable. Something that makes men dislike me, disdain me. What is it? What is so awful about me?

How have I lived like this for so long? Why am I still with this man??? Why is he still here??? What does it matter?

I have complained to You about this and cried out to You about this, but have I really let You fix it? I don't even know anymore. I should just sit with You.

Lord, I am so sorry. Help me, Father. Please heal me. I can't take it anymore.

I am going to claim this scripture:

'You are my Husband. The sorrows of my widowhood, the painful rejection of my husband, the grief I carry over being abandoned by him and all the other men that I looked to I release...But You are truly my Husband. My perfect Husband and the only one who I need. All I ever need is found in Your perfect arms. You have called me back from my grief, with Your never-ending love. It is You who has compassion on me' (my own paraphrase of Isaiah 54)."

THE CORRUPT PATTERN:
WOMEN INTENSELY CRAVE AND MEN RULE OVER

I assume that some of you understand the pain I experienced. Perhaps my words could have come from the pages of your own journal or from your own thoughts. As I read my entry now, I clearly see the intense craving for a man at work in me. I didn't see it then, but I see it now. I took all my deep need to my husband and overwhelmed him with it. I had deep pain and a very broken heart. As always, our good Father responded back to my cry. He told me to go to Hosea 2:13–16. After I read the passage a few times, He told me to rewrite it and He would give me the words, and He did.

As you read, insert your own name. Personalize this passage as much as you need to to make it yours. Read it out loud, and I trust it will be as healing to you as it was to me:

"Susan went looking for her lovers, the men who would fill her heart, and she sacrificed to them. She sacrificed her body, her children, her reputation, her business, her money, her hopes and dreams, and all she had and all she was. She sacrificed all the things that I, her Father and her true Husband, had given her. She poured out all I had given her onto her lovers, only to have them use her and hurt her and abandon her. Susan went looking for her lovers and deserted Me, the true lover of her soul. But I will court her again and will bring her into the wilderness, into the arid places where she will become aware of her pain and her emptiness. I will court her there. As she sits in the awareness of her deep sorrow, I will speak tenderly about how much I love her. I will give to her again: vineyards and fruit and great blessings. And I will restore what she lost, what she spent and sacrificed to her idols, her men. I will open to her a door of hope and welcome her into My love and My care for her. Susan will respond to Me there, and with a heart of joy she will sing to Me, to Me only and not to her lovers. Her lovers and all her idols will be gone, and it will be only her and Me, her true Husband and the lover of her soul. She will love Me again like she did when she first met Me, when she first knew Me, and when I freed her of the pain of sin. I was all she needed then, even if it was just for a brief moment. In that tiny moment of time, Susan looked only to Me. Her eyes were only on Me. I was

all she wanted. Just for a moment. And now, she will return to that love, her love for Me. She will call me 'my Husband,' and she will not remember any of her idols, the empty relationships. She will not even think about running to another man for the comfort and love that she finds in Me. She will finally say to Me, 'You are all I need; You are enough.' I will rejoice with her in that day as it is the day I have waited for, longed for, and desired. It is now here. She is completely mine" (paraphrase of Hosea 2:13–16).

There is an answer for us, and the answer is Him.

5
THE PATH TO RESTORATION

"There is salvation in no one else; for there is no other name under heaven that has been given among men by which we must be saved."
|| Acts 4:12, NASB

"See what kind of love the Father has given to us, that we should be called children of God; and so we are."
|| 1 John 3:1, ESV

"You are passionately loved by the God of the universe. You are passionately hated by his Enemy."
|| Stasi Eldredge[34]

The solution is that everything begins and ends with God. Period. It is really that simple.

However, before we get into that solution in greater detail, let's make sure the problem is well-defined. Because of the fall of mankind, men and women both carry the original sin/pain of the fall. We lost our home, our identity, our purpose, and most importantly, we lost our Father. We are all born into this corrupted design, on a corrupted planet, as abandoned, rejected orphans. Remember that it was the woman who set in motion the circumstances of the Fall and this new corrupted pattern that mankind has reproduced. In her corrupted position, woman intensely *craves after* a man and no longer flows around him with the life and Spirit of God. Until she is healed from it, she will either surrender to this craving for a man, or she will reject it and reject men. Since men and women were created to function as one flesh, to flow and function in tandem, man responds back to her as he was designed to do. He *responds* to her intense craving with the desire to rule over her. That response to rule over is a reaction to her need or her rejection. If he doesn't try to dominate or oppress her, he may respond to her from the opposite end with abandonment and withdrawal. This is the dynamic or pattern of relationship that repeats itself over and over.

As mentioned in chapter 4, this is the root of the conflict in male/female relationships. It is the root of the conflict in most marriages. As marriage and family are the foundation of society, all of society has suffered with the effects of this corrupted pattern. Again, this pattern is now part of our culture; in each generation, it continues on and on. We have been encultured with this relationship pattern to the degree that few of us even question it. We accept that men and women are from different planets, and we don't think beyond that. Yes, we are different, but we are different parts of the same whole, designed to complement each other. The Lord wants to restore us back to this place.

Even though both men and women need to be restored to their original design, the Lord wants to begin by restoring women. As women are healed and are able to function from their original design, men will begin to respond more from their original design, too. Remember, men react or respond to women; so as we change, they will too, whether they intend to or not. It may or may not happen quickly, but it *will* happen. As women encompass men with the Spirit of God, men will eventually revert back to their original design too; the change in men is inevitable.

THE PATH TO RESTORATION

Yet, the focus of this book is on God's restoration of women. The restoration process begins with two things that must be addressed and healed. Both are things we inherited from Eve. First, we need restoration from the *corrupted design* with its new dynamic of relationship. Second, we need our broken and empty *orphan hearts healed*. God must heal our empty and aching hearts that fuel the corrupted dynamic that we carry. This is a spiritual problem, and therefore it requires a spiritual solution. It is only the Lord who can deliver us from the pain and corruption that we inherited. There is no other answer. Only Christ Jesus can set us free (see Romans 7:24; 8:2). He is our Savior, not any other man. In Isaiah 43:11, God declares, "There is no Savior besides Me." God, our Savior, has the solution.

Our answer is found in *relationship* with Jesus, in the salvation He offers us and in the love He pours out on our broken hearts. Restoration and healing are found in relationship with Him, in accepting Him into our lives and hearts. Jesus came and continues to come to seek and save that which was lost (see Matthew 18:11). He didn't just come to seek and save lost *people*; He came to save *everything* that was lost at the fall of man, everything that died and everything that was corrupted. Jesus came to save us from that fate and redeem us to His original plan. Can you imagine if we all lived the way He originally intended for us to live? He wants for us to live free from every consequence of sin and death. Galatians 3:13 says that He redeems us from every curse or consequence, and *all things shall be restored* (see Matthew 17:11). His heart is poised to restore us, as women, to our original design, position, and function. This is critical for our families and our world. Again, it all begins when we receive into our very being what He did for us on the cross. He offers complete healing for our body, soul, and spirit. We cannot be made free without salvation. In the very moment of our salvation, all that was lost at the fall of mankind is reversed and restored to us. We receive it immediately *and* progressively.

Christ's salvation brings us the potential to reclaim everything that is ours, including our original blessed position as women, the encompassers of man and the life-givers. *We do not have to live as slaves to a corruption that makes us crave for a man.* We do not need to be oppressed, in pain and powerless. We were created for so much more. We are the influencers of mankind. We are the source of life on this planet. We are not oppressed, insignificant, powerless women without honor or value. The Lord has come to heal us. He wants to restore us, and He has already provided for our restoration with a Savior.

SALVATION CLEANSES US FROM SIN AND DEATH AND ITS EFFECTS

At the moment of salvation, we become new, and everything that was lost can be restored to us. To receive Christ as our Savior, we simply ask Him to save us. It is not complicated, but it is powerful. It is the answer to everything. The first thing that happens at salvation is that we are cleansed from the corruption we inherited. Every person is born into bondage to corruption caused by sin and death. Had Adam and Eve not fallen, they would have multiplied and created children without corruption, and we would have been born sinless, into a perfect planet surrounded by the Spirit of God. However, that is not what happened. The enemy corrupted their seed before they reproduced. He was then, as he is today, after destroying the next generation. They lost everything, and stood on ground that is cursed. This is what they reproduced.

What we have inherited and what we reproduce is literally and physically a part of us. We cannot live against our corrupted design unless our physical and spiritual self is healed. As Dr. Francis Myles says in his book *The Order of Melchizedek*, "The corruption caused by Sin when it entered the human gene pool caused the prophetic DNA, which God had given to mankind, to mutate. Sin changed the inherent nature of the human genome making it more susceptible to demonic influences rather than the influence of God....Our DNA as humans has mutated to the point that we will never be able to manifest the fullness of the God kind of life in our DNA without requiring a supernatural blood transfusion to flush out all the death agencies (energies) flowing in our bloodline."[35] It is imperative that we recognize the truth of this. We must address this corruption or we cannot be freed. The good news is that this problem is resolved at salvation; the moment we receive Jesus into our hearts and receive His blood, His perfect blood that He shed on the cross restores our very cells. His perfect blood is what redeems us (see Ephesians 1:7, 1 Peter 1:19) and perfects us for all time (see Hebrews 10:14), cleansing us from all sin and its effects (see 1 John 1:7). We are washed clean through Christ's death and the shedding of His blood for us (see Revelation 1:5; 7:14); at that moment corruption is removed from our very blood. Jesus' perfect blood washes our corruption away, and we are healed. At that very moment, we receive it *positionally* and we receive it *experientially* as we grow in Him and appropriate what we have been given.

There is on old hymn that says, "What can wash away my sin? Nothing but the blood of Jesus. What can make me whole again? Nothing but the blood of Jesus." In our corrupted position, we are drawn to think that a man can make us whole, but the truth is that the only thing that can make us whole is Jesus. Men cannot fix us or fill us. Nothing but the blood of Jesus that He shed on the cross washes away all the sin, all the corruption, all the fears, all the rejection, all the hurts, and all the pain. His blood truly makes us whole. He made us whole through salvation, and He gave us back everything else we lost.

If you do not know Jesus as your Savior, all you need to do is ask. Pray with me: "Jesus, please save me from my sins; wash away all the consequences and the pain. Thank You that You died on the cross for me so that I do not have to be bound to death or punished for what I have done wrong. Please restore to me everything that You have already provided. Thank You for saving me and for loving me."

I join with all of heaven, applauding and rejoicing with any of you who prayed that prayer! Welcome to the family and a whole new life with God!

WE GET OUR AUTHORITY, POWER, AND PURPOSE BACK

Adam and Eve also lost all power and authority for themselves and for us when they gave in to the enemy. God gave them all authority over Earth, and they handed it over to the Devil. They forfeited man's right to rule with God over the Earth. God must honor His own word; He gave this authority to mankind and when mankind gave it away, God was bound to that, too. He could not stop them because He would then be going against His own word. Mankind lost our delegated authority, and though He could not stop that, God had a plan to *restore* it back to us — salvation through Jesus. When Jesus was on the Earth, He took authority as a man, anointed by God. He delegated His authority and authorized those with a physical body to have dominion, as He still does today. God does His work on this planet through us. That's why Jesus told us to "occupy" until He returned (see Luke 19:13). "Occupy" means to take possession and to walk in authority. This is what God told man and woman to do in the very beginning (see Genesis 1:26–28): to occupy in His authority. Now, because of Jesus, we can live from our original design today. We can take authority over this planet, and as men and women united together, we can rule as He had planned for us to do. Part of our salvation, what Jesus accomplished on the cross, was the restoration of authority on Earth. Authority wasn't just restored but *won back* by Jesus' death on the cross. He conquered the powers of sin and death and regained all authority (see 1 Corinthians 15:55-57). We now have the potential to function exactly as He intended when He first created us! If we recaptured our original design and reclaimed our God-given authority (see Genesis 1:26–31) and walked in the oneness that couples were created to walk in, then the power and purposes of God would explode on the planet. Nothing would be impossible for us! We have not yet fully achieved this victory because we haven't understood who we really are. But we can be restored to our original design, and we can take back our authority as couples and as a unified male and female army. Even if you just prayed that prayer of salvation moments ago, you too can receive the fullness of the authority He offers to us.

WELCOME HOME

Adam and Eve lost both their physical home and spiritual their home. When they sinned, and were removed from the Garden, Eve lost her place of safety and security. She was sent into the unknown and had to leave her home behind, which was a place of true beauty. She had to leave her spiritual home too; no longer would she dwell with the Father and walk with Him in the Garden, enjoying His glory. She lost her home and our home at the same time. Had they not sinned, all of mankind would have lived, physically, at home in the Garden and lived, spiritually, at home in the presence of God. This loss was tremendous for them and us, as well, especially for women, as we have a deep connection to our home. After my experiences over 20 years of selling real estate, it is clear that most women have more emotions attached to their home than men do! I wonder if we are as emotionally attached to our spiritual home, too?

Because our Father is love and a perfect Father, He wants to restore our home with Him—the Kingdom He made for us to live in—to us. The Lord clearly tells us in Colossians 1:13 that at the very moment we open our heart to Him, He removes us from the kingdom of darkness and brings us *back* into His kingdom, the original home of mankind. We get our home back! God has no homeless children. We have a home, and it is found in Him. We are translated into His kingdom the very moment we receive Him as Savior. The moment we say yes and open our heart to Him, *our home is the Kingdom*! We are made citizens of heaven, and that is where we belong. We can immediately live our life from the Kingdom of heaven, and we are longer subject to the kingdom of darkness or to the emotions of a homeless, orphaned heart. Some of you may not have any connection to the feelings of a homeless orphan that lie deep in your soul. Yet for some of you, the feelings of being lost, disconnected, and homeless are real and tangible. The good news is that no one has to live with that feeling. The Lord wants to heal your heart. Ask and He will. Salvation was designed to give us back all we lost, including our home. When we know Christ as our Savior, He gives us back our home, with Him. We belong in the kingdom of God, of light, and of love. We were created to live in harmony with Him in the beautiful Kingdom He created for us. We can live in the kingdom, our original home, with all that was designed for us. There we can live in our original design as men and women, through our original positions, and with all the good things of the Kingdom of God. This all begins at our moment of salvation.

Once we are saved, and experience salvation, we begin to heal. Our position can be restored to the original design. Everything Adam and Eve lost, we get back. Everything that was corrupted is restored. We are washed from every bit of damage from sin, death, and corruption. We get our authority back. We get our home back. We receive it all at the moment of salvation, yet we need to learn how to appropriate it. We get the keys, but we need to figure out how to drive the car. We get the new clothing, but we need to put it on. We are washed and cleansed, but we need to step out of the mud puddle and stay out of it. This is a process, but once we are saved, we are *free* and *able* to walk out the process. It is immediate freedom as well as progressive. We start by knowing Him as Savior and receiving all He did for us on the cross. Corruption is washed from our design, and all that was lost is restored.

WE BECOME HIS CHILDREN

The day they sinned was the day they became orphans. We can imagine that as she stood at that tree, the first step away Eve took was in her choice to doubt the Father and His goodness. *Maybe He's withholding something from me. Maybe this fruit is okay to eat. Maybe He isn't such a good Father after all.* These may have been the doubts that made her take tiny steps away from the Father of life and love and *into* the arms of sin and death. Her choice to doubt the Father ultimately cost her her relationship with Him, the very relationship that she was deceived into doubting. She lost, and so did all who came after her. We all lost our Father. He is the Father of all who live, have ever lived, or will ever live.

They became orphans, and so did everyone born after them. Our first loss, as we see with the male and female Adam, was the loss of the Father. They carried the seeds of that abandonment, and as Dr. Francis Myles said, this became a part of our human DNA. Galatians 4:4–7 says that Jesus came to redeem us who were *born under the law*; the law of sin and death made us orphans and corrupted our perfect design and our position as women. Our status as God's children, however, is restored to us at salvation. His plan was for us to be restored as His children through the spirit of adoption. This is why He made sure that our salvation would include our adoption as His children. He is the perfect, good Father, and He loves His daughters perfectly. In His love, He made sure to remind us that included with our salvation from sin is a restored relationship with our Father. Jesus says in John 14:18, "I will not leave you as orphans." Romans 8:15 says that the moment we receive Him as our Savior, we receive "the Spirit of adoption by which we cry out '*Abba*, Father.'" The term *Abba* is a deeply intimate and personal term for father; it is more like saying "daddy." He said He will not abandon us; He is our Daddy. He told us to call Him "Daddy," and the relational intimacy that comes with that name is ours as well. He said He would send us Himself so we wouldn't be orphans, and then He *did* send Himself when He sent us Holy Spirit.

Why does He tell us that He will never leave nor forsake us? Why at our moment of being born again does He adopt us? Because that is one of the most critical losses that need to be restored. When we were redeemed, we were also adopted. When we come into relationship with our heavenly Father through the Cross of Jesus, we are no longer orphans. We are no longer fatherless. He is our Father.

Our path to recapturing our original position begins with Him as our Savior; but we must also *embrace* Him as our Father. Our design was corrupted, and salvation restores us from the corruption which that the intense craving we inherited. Yet, that intense craving is partly *fueled* by our orphan heart, which is settled as we embrace Him as our Father. The wound of being orphaned brought us the pains of rejection, abandonment, fear, insecurity, shame, etc. Those wounds and pains caused Eve to turn to Adam, and they cause women today to turn to men; it is the fuel. It is the orphaned heart in us that needs comfort and love. The empty places of our hearts cry out to be filled, the brokenness that seeks for relief. The Lord wants to heal our empty, broken, orphaned hearts because He knows we need it.

Your earthly father may have been neglectful, disconnected, or even abusive. For some of you, it is hard to accept God as your Father. I get that. My father was far from perfect and left many wounds in my heart. I spent years in pain and had a very disconnected relationship with him. Even after I came into relationship with my heavenly Father, the pain from my earthly father was still there. I have had to let the Lord heal me and my "father" wounds that were deep in my heart. For me, it has been a painful and sometimes slow process. But I learned that the best way to fully receive God as my perfect Father was to let Him heal the wounds from my earthly father. I accepted Him as my *Abba*, Daddy. You, too, can bring Him your pain from being orphaned. Let Him heal it, and as He does, you will be restored as a daughter and a woman. For those of you who have/had good fathers and were loved and cared for, it is probably harder for you to be in touch with any place in your heart that is "fatherless." However, until you accept the reality that you inherited the DNA of the original orphans, Adam and Eve, you will not walk in the complete fullness of your restored position. Ask the Father to reveal to you any place in your heart that functions as an orphan. Ask Him to show you any place of rejection or abandonment, or anywhere that needs more love, attention, or affirmation. Ask Him to give you a closer relationship with and revelation of Him as your perfect Father. If you haven't yet received Him as your Father and received the spirit of adoption, then receive it now; ask Him to pour that upon you. Come to Him as His child, His beloved daughter.

I hear the Father saying, "Come away with Me, my beautiful daughter. I chose you before you were born. I created you perfectly. I made you My daughter. I am the Father. I am the perfect Father of life and light and love, and I want to pour out My provision, My care, and My love on you. I want to fill every place in your heart that needs Me. I want you to know that you are My daughter, and all you could ever need is found in Me. I am the only answer for you. I am the only source that can truly fill you. I will touch every place in your heart that was broken, every part of your heart that was ignored, and every part of your heart that is afraid. I want to comfort the precious little girl who didn't know she was loved or cared for or cared about. I heard you. I heard your cries, and I know the places you were hurt. I want to restore your trust in Me and your ability to come to Me as a child, as My little girl. All you need to say is yes. All you need to be is willing. All you need to do is take My hand and come."

Ladies, I hope that you are willing to take His hand and let Him heal you. Please don't stay in the painful corrupt position we have been handed with its obsession of needing a man. Running after men to fill your heart and make you feel loved, special, or beautiful is a trap. It will only leave you yearning for more. If you are one of the women who are hiding from men and rejecting them, this only hurts you. Please allow yourself to step into the original design that He had for you when He created you—as His daughter who can be filled to overflowing with His love. He is your Father who created you to be His child. He designed you to be completely sure of your place as His daughter. You are the *ezer kennegdo*: the powerful influencer of men, the one who is called to fight alongside men as their complementary strength, the influencer and giver of life. You have a voice and a perspective that men need to truly be the best they can be. Bring the deep pain of your orphaned heart to your Father and let Him make you whole.

In these end times, we are seeing the release of more and more of Him as Father. We will look at this in more detail later. For now I want to mention that in Malachi we are told there will be a restoration of the Father and the fathers before the end of the ages. The Holy Spirit is releasing and revealing the Father now. I love the lyrics to some of our songs today that are about the Father. In these lyrics I hear the Father Himself revealing and releasing what He wants: relationship with His children. The spirit of Elijah has come to release the Father over us, removing the orphaned heart that we all inherited, bringing men and women back to their original design and in deeper relationship with their *Abba*.

I love these lyrics from Chris Tomlin's song "Good Good Father."[36]

"I've hear a thousand stories of what they think you're like
But I've heard the tender whispers of love in the dead of night
And you tell me that you're pleased
And that I'm never alone.

You're a good good father
It's who you are, it's who you are, it's who you are
And I'm loved by you
It's who I am, it's who I am, it's who I am

...Oh, it's love so undeniable
I, I can hardly speak
Peace so unexplainable
I, I can hardly think

...As you call me deeper still
into love, love, love
You're a good good father"

WE NEED HIM AS OUR HUSBAND

In order for women to be restored to our original design as encompassers, we also need to receive restoration in our relationship with God as our Husband. When we receive Him as our *Savior*, we are freed from sin, death, and all corruption. When we receive Him as *Father*, our orphaned heart is healed and the pain that fuels our intense craving is alleviated. However, when we receive Him as our *Husband*, our focus changes from an earthly husband to our *heavenly* Husband. As we do this, as we embrace God as our Husband, men cease to be our idols, and God is able to lavish His love upon us in a very intimate way and remove our focus on a man.

Isaiah 54:5 says, "For your Maker is your Husband" (ESV). Hosea 2:16 says, "And in that day you will call me My Husband." Hosea 2:19 says, " I will betroth you to Me forever." Clearly, God wants us to understand and accept Him as our Husband. Jesus is the Bridegroom, and we are His bride. Revelation 21:9 says, "Come, and I will show you the bride, the Lamb's wife." In the third chapter of John, they ask John the Baptist if he is the Christ and he says, "I am not the Christ, but I have been sent before him. And he who has the bride is the bridegroom. The friend of the bridegroom who stands and hears him rejoices greatly at the bridegroom's voice." Jesus Himself says in Matthew 9:15 that He is the Bridegroom. You are Christ's bride, and "Your Royal Husband delights in your beauty" (Psalm 45:11, NIV).

As we've discussed, the woman is the encompasser who creates a circuit of energy around her man and their relationship. That circuit of life energy comes from her connection with God. When she is able to completely connect to the Lord and let His Spirit and His love overwhelm her, a circuit of love and life is created; this is what she can use to encompass man. As Christ's bride, the Lord will meet all her needs and fill her heart with Him. She is thereby able to freely encompass her husband without needing or demanding love from him first. At the Fall, we lost our connection to God and lost our "marriage" connection to Him. Eve lost her intimate connection with Him, as we saw in the consequences from the Fall. Without her God to turn to, she turned to man, as women have done ever since. Again, this is idolatry. Idolatry occurs when we look to anything other than God for provision, comfort, direction or anything else we need or want. It occurs when we look to something or someone to rescue us, fill us, or protect us. It occurs when we value or love anything or anyone more than we value and love the Lord. When we look to a man instead of God, we make man our idol. At the Fall, we were left with a corrupted relationship pattern, which was idolatry. *Idolatry is destroyed when we put God first.*

A few years ago, the Lord gave me a beautiful vision of being married to Jesus. He clearly told me that I was now betrothed to Him and that I was to enjoy Him and look to Him, first, as my Husband. In the months that followed, my earthly husband went through a very stressful time and became increasingly angry. He withdrew and disconnected from me more and more each day. However, most of the time, instead of reacting back to him, I would turn to the Lord. It was a long and painful season that was filled with many opportunities for me to be offended and to be distracted by the pain of my marriage. One day my husband withdrew from me in an especially painful, rejective way and I decided I would pull away from him, too. Immediately the Lord said, "Is that the kind of wife you are?" I replied, "Well, that's the kind of wife I am to *him*." The Lord said, "No, Susan. If you are that kind of wife to him, then you will be that kind of wife to Me also, because that is who you are choosing to be." I was choosing to be the kind of wife who would pull away when she was hurt—no matter who she was married to. I repented. As painful as this season was, the Lord comforted me deeply and loved Me profusely. At times He would refocus me and He would say, "Is he your true husband, or am I?" He would comfort me in keeping me from worrying about what my Earthy husband was or wasn't doing. I was to look to Him first, as my perfect Husband. As I better established my relationship with the Lord, I knew my earthly husband would have no choice but to either be drawn into or repelled by the circle of love and influence the Lord and I were creating. Remember, that atmosphere is magnetic! Unfortunately, my husband did eventually choose to leave—more than once. He would leave and then return only to leave again. It was not the happy life I wanted to experience, but it was what needed to happen at that time. It was *our* process as we allowed God to heal us and our marriage. I learned how to be married to the Lord. I learned that my heavenly, royal Husband wanted to cherish me and lavish love upon me. He was working in me and in my marriage in His way and in His time, and according to how willing I was to go through this process! We must remember that the Lord is not bound to our plans. He is not in heaven waiting for us to say the "right" prayer so He can wave His magic wand and give us the happily ever after ending we want. His purposes are greater, and we must submit our plans to His. His happily ever after for us is far better than anything we can ask for, think or imagine (see Ephesians 3:20). He can be trusted! All we ever need to be is *willing* and *obedient*.

I would like to interject a quick side note. I am not saying that encompassing your husband means that you should accept abusive behavior from him. Nor am I saying that being married to the Lord means we don't "need" our husbands. We do need them and God wants us to. We just don't "need" them instead of God; we don't make idols of our men. What I am saying is that as women, we must first be married to the Lord. He must be our Husband first. As we develop our relationship with Him, we can

THE PATH TO RESTORATION

develop healthy earthly marriages and grow as godly wives. God does not want any of His daughters to be abused. If you are in an unhealthy situation, He will help you. If you or your children are not safe, you need protection. You may need to leave or have your man removed from your home. As you develop your relationship with the Lord, you will hear step by step what to do. Along the way, if you hold onto Him as your Husband, He will cherish you and fill your needs as a wife, even and especially when your earthly husband doesn't. As your Father, He will comfort you when you're neglected and will protect you from abuse. As your Savior, He will deliver you from any evil attacks. The path to restoring your marriage may not look like what you expected and it may not be easy. However, if you don't let go of the Lord, your ending will be good. He is goodness, and all He does is good. Let this be your focus. He is a good God, a perfect Father, and a loving Husband.

Your journey to being restored to your original design begins as you embrace your relationship with Christ and let Him love you. First, accept and receive Him as your Savior. Then allow Him to be your Father and your Husband. Once you do that, you will be able to step more freely into your perfect design and to function as an encompasser. If you do not receive Christ as your Savior, you will not be brought into His Kingdom, nor be able to escape your inner pain, or be washed from all corruption, or function from your restored, powerful position. Without His love, you will not be able to function from your original design. Without His love being your source, you will look for replacements or "idols." You need to experience how He loves you, as His daughter and His bride.

Mother Teresa once said, "The hunger for love is much more difficult to remove than the hunger for bread." Many of us are hungry, many are *starving*, to be loved. The only place any of us has to go to meet the full capacity of our need is to God. We need His love in every relationship role He has with us.

Years ago, the Lord told me that I had limited Him and only allowed Him a business relationship with me—all work, no love. I lived like He was my employer. However, He wanted to lavish His love upon me. For me that was a frightening concept. Love was not something I could easily accept, not from Him or anyone else. In my mind, love meant hurt. Deep inside, I believed that if someone told me he loved me, he would abuse me, betray me, hurt me, or disappoint me. The Lord took me to Proverbs 30:21–23, which begins "Under three things the Earth quakes, under four, it cannot bear up." One of those things is "an unloved woman when she gets a husband." When we haven't been loved and can't receive love, we are unloved women. Other people can try to love us but we will remain fundamentally unloved, because unloved women cannot fully receive love and, most often, no matter how much love is offered, it is never enough, and we can't trust it. Can you imagine what this makes a man feel like when he is trying to love you? If you are an "unloved woman," no matter what he does, it is not enough. No matter how much he is trying, you don't see it, you don't hear it and you won't accept it because you *cannot* until the deepest ache of your heart is settled. Until God settles your ache and fills your need to be loved, you are an unloved woman and, as the scripture says, the Earth itself cannot bear up under you. Unloved women strengthen and continue the corrupt dynamic. We surround men with our need and they cannot bear up under it; we are too much, and eventually they push us away, or in resignation, they give up or maybe even leave. The corrupt dynamic continues. We must have God's love in the deepest parts of our soul. If you are married or single, it doesn't matter—start by embracing the love of the Lord. Receive it. Let Him lavish it upon you.

For some of you, as you disengage from your ache and desire for a man, you will hurt. That ache will feel like loneliness, rejection, unworthiness, and insecurity. So many women have lived with the ache for a man to hold them, cherish them, provide for them, and make them feel safe, secure, beautiful, and complete. When we disengage from our aching need for a man, we are left with the pain of our wounds and an empty place deep inside. All that aching emptiness must be taken to the Lord. Cry out to Him. He is faithful and wants to pour out love on you. It is okay to hurt; no one dies from feeling their pain. The Lord may want you to process the feelings that drove you to chase after a man or even tolerate abuse. He may want you to process feelings from your childhood, or process the feelings of resentment toward your husband for all the things he does or doesn't do. Those feelings most likely need to be felt and processed; and those men will never be the final or complete answer to your internal need to be loved. Maybe they can make you feel loved for a moment, but they cannot make you a *loved woman*. The only answer for you and me is found in the Lord. We begin with His love, because *He is love*. Once we are loved women, we will not make the Earth quake when we are married. Isn't that an amazing description? If the Earth itself cannot handle unloved women when they are married, how can our husbands? Our children? Our cities?

The Lord's love is our source. You need His love to be lavished upon you. His love is so perfect that it will keep you from ever "craving" a man; instead you will be free and able to reach out to a man as an encompasser, full of love, already. God's very substance contains love, and He is the source of love on this planet. Let Him overwhelm you with it. Let Him romance you. I know that allowing Him to love you may be difficult for you. For many years I ran from His love; it was frightening to me. However, He persisted, and over time, I was able to allow Him to love me. Sometimes He would pour out love over me like waves of warmth that went deep into my soul. He will do the same for you. He says that He will! "Your love and beauty chase after me every day of my life" (Psalm 23:6, MSG). He pursues you with His love. In John and Stasi Eldredge's book *Captivating*, there is a paragraph that bears repeating here:

> "Every song you love, every memory you cherish, every moment that has moved you to holy tears has been given to you from the One who has been pursuing you from your first breath in order to win your heart. God's version of flowers and chocolates and candlelight dinners comes in the form of sunsets and falling stars, moonlight on lakes and cricket symphonies; warm wind, swaying trees, lush gardens, and fierce devotion. This romancing is immensely personal. It will be as if it had been scripted for your heart. He knows what takes your breath away."[37]

Seek His love. Accept His love. Rest in His love. Allow His love to be all you need.

His love is what will transform us. As you allow Him to love you, you will be able to pour out that love to others. All love comes from the Father, so any love we have to give came from Him. He is love (see 1 John 4:8). He is the source and the beginning of all love on this planet. First John 4:19 says that we love (only) because He first loved us. Love came from Him. As we receive Him as Father and let His love touch us deep inside, we will disengage from our intense craving for a man and be able to live life as the encompassers we were created to be.

God is not embarrassed to speak words of love to us; just read through the Song of Solomon! "The King has brought me into His chambers" (1:4). "Behold, you are fair, my love!" (1:15). "Rise up my love, my fair one, and come away" (2:10). "You overwhelm my heart with just one glance of your eyes" (4:9). "O my love, you are as beautiful as Jerusalem, turn your eyes away for they have overcome Me" (6:4–5). "Nightly he strolls in our garden, Delighting in the flowers until dawn breathes its light and night slips away. Turn to me, dear lover. Come like a gazelle. Leap like a wild stag on delectable mountains!" (2:17, MSG).

To this we can say, "I am my beloved's and He is mine" (6:3).

The path to restored womanhood is through relationship with Him. He is our Savior who washed away the corruption we inherited. He is our Father and Husband who fills our hearts and makes us whole. In Him, we are loved. He lavishes His love upon us. He overflows our soul with love. We will not crave a man nor make a man our idol when we are intimately and completely lost in Him. In fact, we will not make anything our idol, because He is our everything and we are filled with Him. This is His original design: that we would be in love with Him first and then surrender ourselves to Him and to His plans. Love brings us the power to surrender to Him and to take our place as encompassers. When we experience His loving care, we can let go of focusing on ourselves and our needs and, instead, focus on Him, trusting that all we need is in His care.

SURRENDER YOUR MIRRORS

Once when I was on one of my "I will read the Bible in one year" commitments, I was flying through the latter chapters of the book of Exodus. To me they are a bit boring, and I was trying to get through them and on to the "good stuff" when the Lord stopped me. He said, "You are reading really fast and have missed something very important." I slowed down and read the page again. Still nothing. As I read through it a third time, however, this scripture jumped out at me:

"Bezalel made the bronze washbasin and its bronze stand from bronze mirrors donated by the women who served at the entrance of the Tabernacle."
—Exodus 38:8, NLT

I read this verse over and over and looked at it in several other versions. God revealed to me that this was part of the path to "encompassing the heart of a man."

Let's back up a bit. The last few chapters of Exodus record how the tabernacle of Moses was built, and they list all the objects inside the tabernacle and how everything was made. In the entire record, however, there is only one mention of a specific material that was used to make a specific item—the bronze washbasin. In Exodus there is a record of the people who donated to the project before the artisans and craftsman began their work, and the scripture records the things that were built, sometimes including their dimensions. But I think it is interesting that Exodus 38:8 is the one place in which the Lord highlights that a certain item was built from specific materials. The Lord asked me why He had highlighted this bronze laver, or washbasin, and the mirrors it was made from? I had no idea, but I began to ponder and pray.

Priests used bronze lavers to cleanse themselves before entering the Holy of Holies, the very presence of the Lord. Without being cleansed, the priest could not enter. If a priest carried any stain of sin, he would die in the very holy presence of the Lord. Priests were required to cleanse themselves—to make themselves as pure as possible before entering the powerful, consuming

THE PATH TO RESTORATION

presence of God. The Lord Himself took precaution in preparing the laver for them because He wanted to protect them in His presence and assure that they would be safe. Bells were placed on them so other priests could hear if they were still walking around. If the bells stopped, it would be assumed they were no longer able to walk and the priest would be dragged out of the Holy of Holies by a rope. You see, the laver was life-saving and important to these men. This washbasin allowed them to cleanse and purify themselves in order to protect their lives. This bronze laver was what kept them alive.

And what does the Lord highlight about this cleansing basin? That this incredibly important, life-protecting basin was made from mirrors that women willingly gave for this purpose. He also gives a clue about who these women were. These were women who were on *fire for the Lord*; they were serving, worshiping, and ministering at the doorway of the tent of meeting. The Hebrew word for "served" or "assembled" in Exodus 38:8 actually means "assembled like an army." This army of women was on fire, loving and serving God. They were hanging out in front of the tabernacle and worshiping God as near to Him as their culture would allow. And they *willingly* gave, or contributed, their mirrors. No one forced them to give. They were not taxed. There is no record of them being asked or required to give up their mirrors; they *chose* to give their mirrors so the laver could be built. They chose to give their mirrors so that their men would be cleansed, purified and holy before the Lord.

What did they sacrifice? Their mirrors. It would be a challenge for me to live without a mirror. How would I see how I looked? How would I do my hair or apply my makeup? How would I make myself beautiful? Mirrors let us view ourselves and they help us make ourselves beautiful for men. Women desiring after a man want to look good, and looking good requires having a mirror (or several). But these women were concerned with their inward beauty, not their outward beauty. They were in love with the Lord. This is a key even for today. First Peter 3:3 says that women are not to concern themselves with outward beauty but their inward beauty; this is exactly what *these* women did many many years before Peter wrote these words. I am not saying that doing your hair or wearing make-up is wrong. I am not saying that trying to look your best is wrong. Of course, it is not wrong! *I am saying that to be overly concerned with "me, me, me" is not the attitude of a woman who is going to properly encompass her man.* I am saying that your inward beauty is important, too. I *am* saying to make your focus the Lord and be willing to let Him make you beautiful, inside and out.

In sacrificing their mirrors, those on-fire lovers of God were saying, "I am on fire for my God, and I love Him. I worship Him and am consumed with desire for Him. Because of this, I am willing to give Him all of me. I surrender my view of me, my self-focus, and even my beauty in order for God's men to be purified and holy. I desire for their hearts to be cleansed so they can stand before the Lord in confidence and not fear. I am willing to surrender so the men can be spared and preserved."

When you fully focus on the Lord and allow yourself to be in love with Him and to have all your needs met *by* and *in* Him, your mirror will come from Him too. Second Corinthians 3:18 says, "We all, with unveiled face, beholding *as in a mirror* the glory of the Lord, are being transformed into the same image from glory to glory" (NASB, emphasis added). When you fully surrender to Him, you will see yourself in Him and in His glory. When you do that, it will be easy to surrender your needs and issues. Let go. Let God care for you. Bask in His glory. Release to Him your fears and burdens and hurts. You do not need to focus on them as you focus on His glorious presence. When you see yourself in the glorious presence of the Lord, you will see that you are loved, safe, beautiful, and satisfied. You will be freed from distortions and deceptive perceptions. You will see the you that God sees. You will behold His glory and be transformed by it. A glance into an earthly mirror is a distortion of the real you. The real you is more beautiful than you understand. In Song of Solomon 4:9, God says, "You have captivated my heart, my sister, my bride; you have captivated my heart with one glance of your eyes" (ESV).

These women in Exodus gave up their earthly brass mirrors because their true mirror was the glory and love of God. The Kingdom is often about exchange. We often give up one thing in exchange for another. We trade our sin and shame for salvation. We trade our garments of heaviness for garments of praise and joy. We exchange our fears for faith. We exchange our life for His life. These women gave up themselves and their mirrors in exchange for a new mirror: the glory of the King. They could see themselves in His magnificence. By exchanging their mirrors for His, they saw their true selves *and* they brought an opportunity for their men to be purified and cleansed. The men were purified at the bronze laver and were then able to enter His glory and be transformed by the glory of God, too. What a powerful picture of what encompassing our men accomplishes in their life and ours.

As you surrender to Him, you will be transformed by His glory. God will be your mirror. His glory will be your reflection. He will show you that you are more beautiful than you could imagine. You will not need to intensely crave an earthly man to make you feel beautiful or meet your needs, because God will heal and fill your heart. In that surrender and exchange, you will be able to flow His Spirit around your man. You will be empowered to pray and to guard your man's heart. You can provide an atmosphere for him to choose purity and to be drawn into the presence of the Lord.

This is what the Lord is asking us as women today:

Are you willing? Are you willing to fall in love with Me so deeply that the magnificent, brilliant glory of My presence will be your light and your mirror? Are you willing to behold yourself as in a mirror in the glorious light of My presence? Are you willing to let Me love you and comfort you and define you? Are you willing to let Me be the one who reflects upon you who you are, what you are, and how you look? Are you willing to allow me to define your beauty? Let Me be the one who says that you are captivating. You draw Me into a deep gaze, and I cannot bear to look away for I am entranced by your beauty. Are you willing to let Me be all you need?

Are you willing to see your life in My glory? Are you willing to look at the fears and insecurities of your today and tomorrows within the brightness of My presence? May I be the one who shows you all you are and all you truly have in Me? May I be your mirror to reflect upon you the truth that when you think you have nothing, you have everything? When you are weak, you are truly strong. When you are poor, look again in My mirror, because you will see that you are rich. Look into My mirror, and you will see that your future is filled with hope and all that is good. In My glory, you will see truth. You will see that My love and My life are wrapped around and within yours. No fear or circumstance or hurt or loss can ever define you, because you have been and are defined by Me. In the glory of My presence, you will see that. I will reflect upon you who you are in Me.

Are you willing to let go of your self-focus? The orphan heart is what makes you, My daughter, consume yourself with worry over your circumstances. Your life is in My hands. Your needs are met in Me. Let go of your orphan heart and receive your adoption as My daughter. You no longer need to be concerned about your needs. You are not an orphan without hope, without resources, and without love. You have all and have been given all, and tomorrow you will be given more, and the next day more, and so on and so on, forever. You have more than you need and more than you can imagine.

Will you surrender your mirror and all you see and what you call reality and allow it to be reshaped into something that I can use to heal the man in your world? When you are freed from the burden of self-focus, you will be able to turn to your man without your need. You will no longer ask if you are pretty or desirable or loved, because you will know that you are beautiful and loved and captivating. When you look into My mirror and let go of your own, My perfect love will free you from the burdens of fear. Your fears about your future, your fears of loss and lack, and your "insatiable" needs will be satiated in Me. When you let go of your mirror of self-focus, surrender it to Me and let Me make for him a washing basin, a space for him to hear me, a place for him to be freed and cleansed. Do you see that your surrender will protect and free your man's heart? His heart is unable to carry the fullness of all you need; his heart is not large enough to be your constant source. He is not equipped nor is it his responsibility to completely fill those places in you. When you surrender your mirror and look into My mirror, he is free from all the distractions and the burdens and the condemnation he experienced when he was trying to fill your heart and was not able. Will you free your man from the burden of failure and shame and condemnation? Will you let Me speak to him and fill him and change him and encourage him? I do not place heavy burdens upon the shoulders of my children, but my children do that to each other and to themselves. Be My wife and let Me be your perfect Husband, and I will touch every place in your heart. You are My beautiful bride, and as my wife, I will tell you every day how beautiful you are and how you have captivated Me with one glance. You are my love, my fair one. My eyes rest upon your beauty.

And to Him we will say, Yes! "My lover is mine, and I am his. Nightly he strolls in our garden, Delighting in the flowers until dawn breathes its light and night slips away. Turn to me, dear lover. Come like a gazelle. Leap like a wild stag on delectable mountains!" (Song of Solomon 2:17).

6
WHEN WOMEN ENCOMPASS

> "Don't, by the way, read too much into the differences here between men and women. Neither man nor woman can go it alone or claim relationship priority."
> ‖ 1 CORINTHIANS 11:10–11, MSG

> "All this comes from the God who settled the relationship between us and Him, and then called us to settle our relationships with each other."
> ‖ 1 CORINTHIANS 5:18, MSG

I love how 1 Corinthians 5:18 reads in *The Message* Bible. God settled our relationship with Him at the cross, and now, at our own crosses, we settle our relationships with each other. He *already* gave women and men everything we need to settle our relationships with each other; we just didn't know it. He *already* provided a solution, and now it is up to us to do our part. Women can pick up our cross, reclaim who we were created to be and in that settle our relationship with men. We must not forget that reclaiming our original design will require spiritual help. We cannot just decide to reclaim our original position and set out to do that using our own will power and intelligence; it requires the Spirit. In His presence, the Spirit *will* transform us back to who we were designed to be. I love how our foundational scripture, Jeremiah 31:22, reads in *The Message* Bible. It says that when we embrace our transforming God, then we are transformed. Being transformed begins with embracing Him, our transforming God, and receive Him as our Savior, our Father, and our Husband. As He pours out His love on us, we are transformed and freed. As we are transformed by His love, we are empowered to take back our position as encompassers. As we focus on Him, surrender to Him, focus on His ability to meet our every need, and let Him love and define us, we are freed to be who we were created to be. All we must do is be *willing*, and He will restore. We just need to say yes to Him. Be willing and obey. Embracing our transforming God can truly transform us and settle our relationships.

If you followed the steps in the last chapter to receive Christ as your Savior, Father, and Husband, then you are on the path of a truly transformed woman! As you grow in Him, and grow closer to Him, you will transform more and more into His original design for you as a woman. As you surrender yourself to Him and His plans and His lordship over your life, then you *will* look to the Lord instead of a man to make your life better and happier. I realize it is not easy, but it is simple, and those simple steps in chapter 5 contain the answer to reclaiming your original design and its inherent power.

Even though this chapter is directed more to the married women, yet, for single women, you can benefit too. As single women, for those who do want to marry one day, this is your time to prepare and get ready. Be completely freed from your intense craving for a man. Become a loved woman. You can be so settled in the Lord, that He, as your Husband, is all you truly need. As you stay in the flow of you and the Lord, I truly believe you will draw in the right man. If you stay in this life with the Lord, fully loved and loving Him, He will help you to understand your position to encompass. You will begin to look at men differently. When you view a potential husband, you will ask better questions: How much work will it take to keep a flow of the Spirit around him? How much work will it be to stay unoffended, to stay in the flow in the Spirit, and to keep from becoming bitter? How often will you need to forgive him—or, better said, how considerate, kind, and loving is he? How hard will it be to pray this man into his calling and purpose? How far is his heart from the Lord, and what will be required of you to keep the Spirit flowing around him? How much will you have to surrender, and will he surrender the same? And the biggest question: if he is not in love with the Lord, how will the two of you be able to rule and reign together? A man might say the right words but not have the right heart. If you are still full of your old corrupted design, the pull of your intense craving can draw in the wrong man for you and at the wrong time. Remain clear and focused about what you're committing to. Life is hard enough already without adding a future with broken relationships or a marriage full of extra work for you. While all relationships require work, you don't need to do *unnecessary* work. Find a man who will make your part easier, and even pleasurable. Find a man who you want to sacrifice for and a man you *want* to encompass. Keep your circle of you and the Lord strong and healthy, then you will simply accept him into the circle you've already created to form another "circle," the circle of a marriage covenant.

Last, for the single women, especially those who are not considering marrying, these principles and concepts are applicable to all women. You can still apply these concepts to all your relationships with men, the concepts are the same but the level of intimacy is less. It is true that the marriage relationship contains a greater of depth of intimacy and spiritual power. The sanctity and power within the covenant of marriage is certainly more complex than other relationships. The ability to function as one flesh was created for marriages, exclusively. However, every woman can use these principles, to some degree, in their relationships with any man. Our design is the same. Please, single women, continue with this chapter and apply the ideas and concepts.

For every woman, married or single, the foundation for this restoration to your position of power rests upon your relationship with the Lord. As you maintain your connection to the Lord and do not break that flow of His Spirit, you will either draw men to that energy or they will choose to be repelled. This is how electricity works: when electrons move through a wire, they create a magnetic field and, depending on their charge, two wires placed near each other will either attract or repel.[38] Similarly, the Lord is a Spirit consisting of energy or a field of electricity. The electromagnetic field of His Spirit draws us to Himself. Jesus says He will *draw* all men unto Himself (see John 12:32). In John 6:44, Jesus says that no one can come to Him unless the Father *draws* them unto Him. In James 4:8, we are told to draw near to Him, and He *will* draw near to us. This is the magnetic force of the Spirit of God.

RESTORED WOMEN RELEASE THE SPIRIT

As we are transformed, we can fulfill the other dimensions of Jeremiah 31:22 to become women who encompass our men. In chapter 2, we learned we were created to encompass from within the internal world of our men. Before woman was a living soul inside man, she was in the heart of our Father, our Creator. *He contained us first*, and we were part of His female expression. Think of what that means for us today. As we connect with His heart through relationship and loving surrender, we reconnect to His heart and can connect His heart to our men. We start our transformation as we love God first. We do not need to force ourselves into a man's heart, nor do we need to beg or plead for entrance into a man's heart. When we let go of our intense craving, we stop those demanding behaviors. We are freed from wondering if we are loved, and our hearts are settled. Just as *God placed woman inside man* to surround his heart, He can do the same for us today. He can put us "inside" a man where we can be safe, loved, protected, and cherished. I love Proverbs 21:1: "The king's heart is in the hand of the Lord...He turns it wherever He wishes" (KJV). The NIV translation says He "channels [it] toward all who please him." God can direct the flow to turn a man's heart toward you and place you within it.

As encompassers of our men, we make a circuit, and hopefully we make a circuit of life and not death. We are a "source of life" to our men when we enter into God's Spirit and flow with Him, and we can draw (as an electromagnetic force) our men into that flow. I believe that this is partly why we can "win over our husbands without a word" (1 Peter 3:1–2). How powerful it is to encounter the Spirit of God! He is the very power of life. Wherever He flows, His power overcomes. In His flow, in the flow of His river, the rivers of living water that flow from inside us, the dead are brought back to life, the sick are made well, and evil and darkness are overwhelmed with good. It is time to embrace the power He has bestowed upon us.

We have an amazing design. We are able to connect with His Spirit and to create an atmosphere around our men to draw them closer to Him. As mentioned in chapter 2, there is scientific evidence to prove that the energy field we have as humans allows us to encompass. The heart generates a considerable amount of electrical energy; it is the most powerful generator of electromagnetic energy in the human body. The electromagnetic energy of the heart not only envelops every cell of the human body, it also extends in all directions around us and can affect others' brainwaves. This is called heart-brain synchronization.[39] The heart can reason, think, and communicate to those around it with an electromagnetic field of energy. Here again is a picture of how we were created. I love when science proves God and gives us a better understanding of His handiwork. *We came directly from the power-filled heart of God, then were placed inside man to surround his heart.* We were made in His image as a multidimensional being that is connected in unity with a powerful flow of energy that draws men toward the energy we are sending.

I want to make sure you understand how crazy powerful our position is as women! Women can encompass men with death, bitterness, and nagging, or we can be intimate with the Spirit of God and encompass them with a powerful circuit of life. Then they respond to whatever energy we surrounded them with. We can surround them with life or death. When we live close to God's heart, we have more of Him and His Spirit to give. In Him, we are more and we can *do* more than we can imagine! We cannot do it on our own, but we can do it as we stay *in Him*. We can only encompass with life and function in our correct capacity when we encompass our men using God's power. When we are filled up with God's love and life-giving power through Christ, we encompass with power. We need to embrace who He has made us and how He has made us and understand our responsibility to carry this love to our men and to our world! What a world we can create!

DAILY REAL-WORLD ENCOMPASSING

I recognize that I'm using very esoteric terms. It may be helpful to examine the concept of encompassing as it applies to more practical, real-world situations.

Let me give you a comparison.

Say that you are a woman who is not functioning from your original design. Perhaps you have no idea who you were created to be. To some degree, you are functioning from the corrupted design, because until it is healed, the corrupted design is how all women function. Let's say that you are also married and are facing some challenges. You see some things that you think your husband needs to do or stop doing, and you think that he is making the other issues you're facing worse. Maybe he is even the cause of the issues! You worry that if these issues don't get resolved soon, your children, your finances, or your marriage will suffer. You imagine the fearful things that could come from these unresolved issues: financial ruin, divorce, and negative effects on your children. Without deep connection to the Lord, your unmet needs, wounds, and fears take over and determine how you live, speak and act. You come to your husband with *that* flow — with the energy of your fears, your insecurity, your intense emotions, and your overwhelming needs. Oftentimes these deep issues are disguised as irritation with your husband, criticism, hurt feelings, complaints, resentments or demands. That is what you encompass him with. As the one who is "intensely craving" him, you surround him with your sin and death-filled energy; you look to him as the solution. You are seeking relief from your brokenness. Then he responds to your intensity and the spirit you have surrounded him with from his corrupted position, from his fallen state as a fearful orphan. You have encompassed him with your need and with your intense desire for him to relieve your emotional pain. Your unmet needs *translate* as problems that you want him to fix, something you want him to change, pain you want him to comfort, or an answer you want him to supply. He responds to you as one who is your counter-part, designed to respond in tandem as one flesh with you. He responds to your energy and wounds from his wounds with the same energy. Your brokenness attracts his brokenness and he responds. Deep down inside, far below his conscious mind, he fears he cannot meet your needs or solve your problems. He responds from his corrupted design and "rules over" you. He blows up in anger, or accuses you of overreacting, or blames you for the problems. He overpowers you with attempts to shut you up. Or perhaps he goes to the other end of the continuum and he hides. He says he'll talk about it later, but later never comes. He hides from you by getting away and staying away from you and the issues you are concerned about by watching TV, overworking, or simply shutting you out. As this flows back to you, you flow back to him with more irritation and resentment. You are left with the unresolved problems you started with, and now you have more hurt. All of this works to keep you both disconnected from the Spirit of life. If you know the Lord, but haven't understood your design, then you turn to the Lord to complain. If you don't know the Lord, you may take your complaints to your friends. *Why isn't your husband a stronger man? Why is he so clueless? Why doesn't he take care of things? How can he ignore these problems? Why does he ignore you?* You feel justified in your complaints and demands and criticisms. You may cry to the Lord to fix or change your husband, but until you recognize the corrupted design in action, you pray and ask for the wrong things.

Let's examine the same scenario, but this time say that you are a woman who is aware of who you are as encompasser, and you know the Lord deeply and intimately, and you look to the Lord to meet your needs and to be your Husband and Father. In this scenario, your family is facing some challenges. You know that these issues need to be resolved. You begin by going to the Father and your perfect Husband. You pray. The Lord comforts and settles you. He alleviates your fears, and your healed heart no longer reacts from the heart of an orphan. You know you are His daughter. You also know that He is in control, and you know that you are the one who influences your husband. You press into the

Holy Spirit, and you create the atmosphere that surrounds you, your husband, and your home with the Spirit of life. The Lord may have given you some insight to how your husband is feeling about these issues or He may have given you a strategy for how to speak with him. This is your design, and you have chosen to function from it. Already, the situation is dramatically different: you have some measure of peace, you are in unity with God, you have an understanding, He has calmed your worries and fears, He has addressed whatever fears or wounds may have been stirred in you. He has settled your heart and you are not being controlled by your emotions. You do not need to obsess and fear about your life, your finances, your children, or whatever you think you need. You know that the Lord has everything under control, and you know your place of power is to surround your husband and your marriage with a peaceful, life-giving Spirit. Now, when you come to your husband, the flow is different and communication is different. You no longer "intensely crave" him or look to him first; you already went to the Lord. You do not attack your husband with your needs or your pains or your fears. You are not irritated because you recognize that he is neither the root of the problem nor the solution. You bring the flow of the Spirit to the situation and to him. Your husband reacts differently because you encompassed him with the Spirit of life and he will respond back to you with some measure of the Spirit. Even if he is emotionally unhealthy or far from the Lord, his response will be somewhat restrained because he is surrounded by the Spirit of God. If he chooses any sort of unhealthy response, it will be diminished from what it could have been, because the Holy Spirit restrains evil, and you have created a flow of God to surround both of you. In any case, you can be at peace. The situation is different because you surrounded your husband with the Spirit, not the intensity of your need. At best, he will come under the influence of the Spirit and will respond from the Spirit. At worst, he will be restrained. If he were able to understand your design and his—if he functioned from his original design as your container, protector, and leader—this scenario would be even better. From the position of his original design, he would listen. He would understand that he needs to hear from you, that your perspectives are valuable, and that life depends on the two of you functioning together. Because you encompassed him with life, he would respond back to you with life. Together you would be able to solve problems and communicate in peace. Together you could appropriate the creativity and the power inherent in your design and take dominion over the circumstances of your lives.

This example may seem oversimplified, but it is not. Every marriage could look like this, because this is how we were designed to function—in the peaceful unity of the Trinity. This is our design, and we can recapture it. As you enter into this life of an encompasser, the Spirit will help you no matter how your man responds. If you choose, you can be strengthened so you are no longer offended. You can be strengthened to be able to forgive. You can be empowered to continue to surround him with the Spirit of life. The Lord, your Husband, can and will help you. He will give you strength. I know this is hard, but since I have done this, I know you can too. It may be difficult to recover our lives, our men, and our families, but it is the best option. As long as you choose to operate from your original design, you will never suffer the difficulty of the first scenario. Even if it is only you who has revelation of the original design and chooses to live from it, you will still experience a better way of life, with a promise from God that the end will be good. Eventually, your actions will create change.

In His Word, God has shown us how we are designed to function in unity like the Trinity. Through science, He has shown us how our brains were created to function best together, like the Trinity. He has shown us how electricity works and its powerful magnetic pull, which draws in, the same way that He draws us.

Eventually, at some point, your husband will be drawn into your flow or he will be repelled. Even the most difficult situations can be restored. Again, the Lord does not want His daughters to functions like doormats or victims. Instead, He wants you to be powerful victors and leaders. You *can* and you *will* function from a whole heart rather than from your pain. You will speak truth and love and you will flow with the Spirit of God. Some of you may need to create healthy boundaries, find your voice, and take back your life. The Lord may direct you to create temporary boundaries to protect you or your children, especially if there is abuse or addiction involved. However, no matter the circumstances or situations, you are directed to encompass your husband, and you can trust that this process will lead to an expected end, a future, and a hope (see Jeremiah 29:11). You will grow into your position as a powerful giver of life and an encompasser of mankind. This is the position from which you will rule and reign with your husband.

Your original design is rooted in a powerful place in the spirit realm. To be restored to that powerful place and reconciled to your husband require a spiritual solution because it is a spiritual problem. Total reliance on Him and His presence is your spiritual solution. Restoration requires that you enter the flow of the Spirit of God, and His Spirit will help you grow and transform. Jeremiah 31:22 tells us that transformed women *embrace* their transforming God. We don't just glance His way once in a while, occasionally read His Word, and send up a short "help me" prayer when we're in trouble. No, an embrace requires holding on. He is our life, so we don't let go of His presence. This requires practice. Practice the presence of God daily. Make it your focus. Stay away from the things that grieve and hinder His presence. Make hosting His presence your first priority.

The Bible is clear that the number one thing that stops the flow of His Spirit in our life is unforgiveness (see Matthew 6:5–

15; Matthew 18:21–35; Mark 11:22–26). If you choose to be offended, you lose the fullness of His presence, your ability to correctly encompass is compromised, and the Enemy wins again. When you choose to stay offended and refuse to forgive, you block your access to His Spirit, and the flow around your husband is no longer that of the Spirit of God; instead, it is a flow of resentment and anger. When you complain to your girlfriends about your man, when you hold onto resentment, or when you blow up in anger from your offended heart, you disconnect from the source of life and create a new flow without God in it. You block the flow of the Father's love and life. This is the corrupted design in action, repeating the dynamic that you don't want. Eve disconnected from the source of life and chose death, and then she encompassed Adam. When he ate, the circuit was complete, and death energy became their new flow. Do you want to flow life or death? It is a simple choice, but it is not an easy one. Staying in the presence of God and resisting all that hinders His presence are hard work.

There was a season in my life in which the Lord was trying to teach me how to encompass. He showed me that I was not allowed to be offended, not even for a moment. He wanted me to stay conscious and aware of every moment. In the following few months, my husband moved out and was saying that he wanted a divorce. He often said very hurtful things and there were countless opportunities to be offended every day, justifiably offended, in my opinion! But the Lord reminded me that if I chose to be offended, then I would be unable to encompass my husband with His Spirit. I could either stay mad at my husband, or I could stay in His presence; I could not have both. I had to, moment by moment, choose forgiveness and choose to stay unoffended. During this time, the Lord showed me some parts of my husband's heart that had been traumatized as a child. The Lord showed me that from these broken places, he was choosing addictive behaviors to push down his pain. God showed me how desperately my husband needed mercy. He directed me to pray for His mercy to be poured out on my husband in these areas. When I began to pray, He stopped me and said that I needed to do something first. He showed me I couldn't come into the court of heaven and ask the Judge for mercy when I still had so much unforgiveness in my heart. First, He said, I needed to deal with my offended heart. Then and only then could I enter the court and ask for mercy for my husband. Working through the issues—some that I had long forgotten and buried deep in my heart—was a process. But He helped me through the healing, and then I went freely into the court and asked for mercy for my husband. God did answer that prayer, and He brought some healing to my husband. This all started with me letting go of my resentments.

Letting go of unforgiveness and encompassing your husband's heart with prayer is powerful. This especially requires that you stay in His presence. When we are hurt and offended, the last thing our flesh wants is to forgive. What we *feel* like doing often looks like revenge, angry outbursts or demands for apologies. Forgiveness is not something we can do in our own strength or with our will power. If you are struggling with unforgiveness, please read the book *The Bait of Satan* by John Bevere; I think it is one of the best books on this subject. Let God help you so that you do not grieve Him. The end of chapter 4 of the book of Ephesians provides an outline for what grieves the Holy Spirit. Anger, wrath, and malice are just a few. I am sure I am not the only woman who has embraced some of those. When we hold onto those, we cannot be in the Spirit, and we cannot encompass with anything but our offended, resentful and unforgiving spirit. That chapter of Ephesians ends with an encouragement to "be kind and compassionate to one another, *forgiving* each other just as Christ *forgave* you" (NIV, emphasis added). A forgiving and unoffended heart is critical to staying in the presence of the Holy Spirit. When you are able to flow around your husband with the

Spirit and not from a place of resentment-filled irritation, he will have the opportunity to respond in the Spirit.

PRAYING FOR HIM IS ENCOMPASSING HIM

The last story leads me to the next point: part of encompassing your man is prayer and intercession for him. You were designed to surround his heart, as part of his rib cage; you are there as a guard. Proverbs 4:23 says we are to guard our heart with all diligence for from it flows our life. Our desires, fears, affections, dreams, feelings, etc., flow from our hearts. All of who we are flows from our hearts. We are positioned in man's chest to be an influencer and to guard the issues of his life and all that comes from his heart. As we saw in chapter 2, even science proves that we were made with brains that are wired to sense our hearts and theirs. We *can* understand men, at times more than they understand themselves. We are near their hearts to watch, to discern, to interpret, to influence, and, most importantly, *to pray*. We have this responsibility and ability to support our men. We were designed to understand their hearts and to use that knowledge for their good—not to judge, shame or manipulate them. Be respectful and careful. You have been invited to be close to their heart; don't take that lightly. As you pray, that prayer flows the Spirit around their hearts. First Thessalonians 5:17 says, "pray without ceasing." Ephesians 6:18 says, "Pray in the Spirit at all times." Colossians 4:2 says, "Devote yourselves to prayer." Watch the movie *The War Room*, and you will be motivated to pray! Married or single, pray. If you are waiting for a husband, pray for him now! You *are* designed to surround and guard man's heart by encompassing him with prayer and intercession and they need us to.

What if every woman interceded for the men of the world? How strong would the men of the world be and what would our marriages look like if we were able and willing to intercede daily? Not only married women, but all women need to pray for our men. We all need to pray for our sons and brothers and fathers. We hold valuable insight into their hearts and their lives that can move the mountains that stand in their way when we pray. Selflessly seek to understand and, through prayer, influence the flow of men's hearts. Pray for the Lord to touch their wounds, to remove their fears, and to give them what they most need. You surrendered your mirror, now continue to be a part of the purification for them. Pray for cleansing and for purity, that this world would not stain our men. Pray for their hearts to be free from lust and pray for cleansing for their sexuality. Pray for courage and confidence. Pray for our men to be holy before the Lord.

Wives, pray that the Lord would reveal the deep things in your husband so you can be there in the deep places of his heart. That is true intimacy. This is what your husband needs from you, and he will honor and value you for it. A man who can feel safe with you and trust you with his heart is a man who will cherish you. Adam was aware of how valuable Eve was to him. He knew what she did for him internally. He knew what she supplied for him. But most men of today have no idea who we are to them or what we supply. Many of them do not know what they are missing from us. When I hear some women complain about how clueless men are, I encourage them to do their job of connecting to the Lord and pray in the flow of the Spirit so their men can get a clue. If your man is clueless, don't judge him, don't shame him, don't complain to your friends about him, and don't stay frustrated. Instead, repent and pray for him—pray for what his heart is missing. Read chapter 5 again, and ask the Lord to help you. You need to be transformed to be able to encompass him with life and love, and when you are, he will honor you. He wants to trust you with his heart. Consider for a moment the story of Sampson and Delilah. We know that she did many things to him that were not godly, but one thing she did is a good example for us. Delilah provided a place for Samson to lay his head. He was able to find rest with her. From that place of rest, he let her into his heart and told her all of his secrets. Granted, she misused that, but the point is that *he poured out his heart to her*. I believe that this is because it is the design of a man: he wants to share his heart with you; on some level he knows you belong there. As you stay close to the Lord and let Him love you, a space is created for your man to lay his head, open his heart and tell you his secrets. I promise.

This task to intercede for them requires that you stay very close to God as your Husband. I know this can be hard, but I am not asking you to do something I have not done, and if I can, you can. For those of you with difficult marriages, you, especially, will need a real relationship with Him to sustain you, heal you, and keep you away from both codependent victim attitudes or angry explosive attitudes. It is a new way of life and those old mindsets won't serve you anymore. They are part of the corrupt design of "needing" and demanding your man to take the ache away. Let the Lord stay close as your Husband. He has often validated my hurts, without letting me keep my bad attitudes, while reminding me that He too desires for me to be cherished. The Lord wanted my husband to cherish me the same way He cherishes me. The Lord reminded me that one day my husband would be able to do that, even though that day hadn't come yet. He reminded me that if I let Him fill my need to be loved and cherished, I would not be desperate for my husband to fill that role. He reminded me of the path to restoration—explaining that if I stayed on this path, my husband would either be drawn into the flow of His Spirit or he would leave. Again, as I said, my husband did leave me along the way, not just once but twice. Choosing to live as an encompasser is not a quick fix. You can't just wave a magic wand and make everything better. What I am saying is that it is a process. It might be long. It might be painful. Your process may look different than mine, but one thing is for certain: you need God as your Husband to love you, comfort you, and show you each step to take. You will need Him as your Savior to deliver you and give you strength. You will need Him as your Father to protect and provide for you. The process requires that you remain in Him, that you stay unoffended, that you hold onto the power of forgiveness, and that you follow Him as He shows you each step to take. He has a plan, and it is far better than yours. His ways are higher than yours. Embrace His plans, and surrender your mirror, that burden of me, me, me! For a time, you may have to be the one to do the hard work; you may be the *only* one to do any work. That is a hard walk and will require some crying at the feet of the Lord and some difficult choices, but if I can do it, you can too. The power of the Lord will flow through you as you choose to forgive and choose to not be offended. You will be strengthened to submit to the process and to surrender to the Lord's purposes. Your intercession for your husband will change from asking for the things that will make *your* life better; it will become true intercession that will prepare *him* to follow the Lord's purposes for *his* life.

DO THE MEN IN YOUR LIFE FEEL LIKE A FAILURE?

One day, I was sitting in a worship session at the Healing Rooms in Santa Maria, enjoying the worship and the beautiful presence of the Lord that was filling the room. The Lord clearly said, in an almost audible voice, to turn to Amos 4:1. I did immediately and started to read, "Hear this word, you fat cows who lie on the hills of Bashan..."—I said, "What? Are you calling me a fat cow?" The Lord told me to continue reading—"...who demand of their husbands, I am thirsty, bring me another drink." I continued through that passage, and the next verses talk about idolatry. I was not sure what to think of this. Then the Lord began to speak to me. He said, "You have made your husband your idol. He is your source; you look to him to fill you. You turn to him and demand that he meet your needs and quench your thirsts for love and attention." I responded by arguing. Of course, I denied it, saying I didn't demand anything from my husband. He responded, "Yes, you do. Reflect on the times when you get angry about what he *doesn't* do for you. Those are the things that you have, deep inside, demanded from him." I knew this was true. At that word, I began to cry and repent. The Lord reminded me that it is impossible for my husband to meet all of my needs. I repented of the idolatry, and I asked Him to be my Husband. I vowed to look to Him first. He began to show me that it isn't my *husband's* job to meet all my needs; it is *His*. Second, my husband couldn't meet my needs if he tried—even if he were the best Earthy husband—because he can't meet the deep ache of my soul. *Even a great husband still makes for a weak god.* Then the Lord asked, "Do you know why I am saying you are as a fat cow?" He showed me that I know Him, that I hear Him, and that I have free access to Him. He showed me He can meet every need I bring to Him. My spirit was as a fat cow, because although I was able to receive His love in my spirit and from there pour it out on others, I refused that in my own soul. I kept my soul away from Him and His love. I knew His love in my *spirit*, I was full with His love, but my own *soul* was full of hurts and pains that I wasn't dealing with. I kept the Lord from entering those empty, broken places; instead, I turned to my *husband* with them. The middle of the Amos 4:1 scripture says, "You oppress the poor and crush the needy." This is what I was doing to my own needy soul. My soul was poor and needy and I ignored that, pushed it down, crushed and suppressed it, instead of letting the Spirit of God pour from my spirit into my own soul. Instead I demanded of my husband to fill me. Of course, I did not realize

I was doing this. It was not conscious on my part at all. But as the Lord brought me this truth, I had no other response than to agree with Him and to repent with great tears. He then showed me that when I demanded that my husband satisfy my thirst for love and affection, I made my husband feel like a failure. Since he couldn't meet my need, he would feel the pain of failing me. Again, not consciously, but deep inside he felt like he was failing me because he was; he could not completely meet my needs nor fully remove my ache. The Lord said, "You are making My son feel like a failure every day, and I cannot allow you to do that." I know that I am not alone in this. I trust that some of you will see some of yourself in this story. I trust you will repent, too. We don't want to, but nonetheless, we make our men feel like failures when we expect them to meet our every need.

During this time, I did not have the full revelation of this book, or of the Fall, and I did not recognize that this was the corrupted relationship pattern in action. Eventually, I saw it. When I turned to my husband with my thirst and intense craving to be loved, when I was driven by the "desire after" him and I encompassed him with it, demanding that he meet my needs, this is the corrupt dynamic in action. In this circuit or circle I created, my husband felt his inability to meet my needs. I am sure he didn't *consciously* realize this, but somewhere deep inside, he felt it. I flowed around him with my need, which I turned into demands and judgments and criticism, asking him why he didn't listen, why he didn't care, and why he didn't love me. He responded back by getting defensive, by yelling at me, or by withdrawing and ignoring me. The Lord had me walk this out for months, keeping me very aware of this pattern, showing me when I was turning to my husband with my thirst. As I walked this out, this is when the Lord began to explain the consequences we received at the Fall. He revealed to me my intense craving and idolatry. He showed me the corrupted dynamics of men's and women's relationship patterns. He showed me that my husband would not open his deep places to me if encompassed him with my need and the message that he was a failure.

You cannot intimately surround a man's heart if you are consumed with yourself and your own emotional needs. If you are consumed by your own fears, you cannot encompass his heart with life and love. I understand, though, that brokenness in our hearts drives us toward something with skin, someone we can see; it seems easier to turn to a real person sitting near us for comfort. But, again, you are surrounding him with your need. The only real place any of us have to go is to the Lord. He is the One who loves you perfectly. Without that connection, without God's love, you have nowhere to go to solve your own inner ache. We all need to be loved, to know we are beautiful. We all need to know we are worth fighting for, worth listening to and worth being loved. We need attention and affection and comfort. I am not saying to ignore those things, or deny them, I am saying to take them to the Lord; let Him take care of you. When your emotional needs are met by our perfect Husband and Father, then you can surround your man without your needs. When your heart is settled in Him, you can pray for your husband's heart without manipulating. You can influence him without controlling. You can guard his heart without demanding. In the places that he fails, you can pray for his repentance without shaming him. Will you flow around him with shame, resentment, bitterness, criticism, and a long list of needs for him to fill? Or will you choose to be the daughter and wife of the King and to encompass your husband from a love-filled heart? Will you encompass your man with God's Spirit?

SUBMISSION

"Can two walk together, except they be agreed?"
—Amos 3:3, KJV

The concept of submission is probably one of the most misinterpreted, misunderstood, and misused concepts regarding marriage. What has happened to women from this very misconstrued subject is, in my opinion, one of the Christian church's greatest errors. Telling a woman she must "submit" to her husband has often caused women and their children to be abused, mistreated, and left as frustrated, powerless victims. Many of us have been taught that men are in charge, that God made them to lead, and that we should be quiet, submissive helpers. We have been told that women should not fight for control but should follow men as our leaders, no matter how they lead, or don't. This is the picture of "submission" that I have read in books and been taught by many church leaders over the years. Maybe you have, too. However, the real concept of submission is truly beautiful and full of power.

In the introduction, we looked at the Law of First Mention, which states that the first mention of something is where you find the most basic and purest form of its design. From that basic design, you add the more complex, staying within the basic design. Using this principle, we take the basic concept of how men and women were created and designed as the foundation; then more complex concepts like "submission" can be added. With that thought in mind, we can understand why the concept of "submission" has been taught so wrong! It is based on a faulty design—the supposed truth that only Adam was made in God's image and that Eve was sort of an afterthought; that Eve was created to alleviate Adam's loneliness and to be his assistant to help *him* rule and reign; that after the fall, women became power hungry and wanted control. Building from this design, it is assumed that women, as mere helpers, should submit to men, who are superior and better rulers. The idea of submission here is awful and it's a lie that makes it seem like men have all the power and women have no power. We know now that this is not the picture of how men and women were created to function, and it is certainly not the true picture of submission.

Many women have stayed in abusive, unhealthy marriages because we thought it was how we were supposed to submit. I was taught that submission meant giving my husband all control and all decision-making power. I acted and prayed from these places of powerlessness and expected God to move on my behalf, which seemed reasonable and even scriptural. Then, one day, the Lord began to change His response to me and my prayers. He stopped acting on the things that I was praying for and the things I was asking Him to do for me in my marriage, things that even seemed to be in alignment with His Word. You see, my understanding was far from God's original design. I am so glad that He pulled back and left me to question. He began to reveal to me that if He had continued to answer my prayers and bless my efforts the way I thought He should, I would have kept believing and accepting the error. Instead, He had a bigger plan. He wanted me to seek after truth, which was more important than any momentary relief in my marital problems. He wanted me to understand the real truth and its true power. I began to understand that the concept I had believed about submission was completely wrong, and I needed to let go of all my wrong ideas about marriage!

Women were never intended to just be quiet and go along with whatever men say or do. Mankind was created as equal partners to rule and reign, and women have an important role to play. It is from these concepts that we must apply the Law of First Mention, from the true picture of men and women. This way, we can build a complex concept of submission on a more accurate foundation.

Here is the foundation we will build on: God made mankind in His image; He made male and female in one body. Together with the Lord, mankind was as the Trinity. Each part had its own functions. Male contained, protected, and housed the female. Female, a soul living inside male, surrounded his heart, communicated to him from deep within, kept watch of his heart, and flowed around him with the Spirit and with life. Female was designed to live most productively in this internal world of the senses, the spirit and intuition. Male, with his eyes and ears, was designed to live most productively and comfortably in a tactile, physical, clear-cut world. (Men can be internal and sensitive, and women can certainly think logically, but as we have said many times previously, this is how male and female were originally designed.) Male and female were to join their different strengths and positions and make choices, take action, and reign over their world, *together as one*. They were to appreciate and appropriate their differences and strengths, knowing they needed each other to function as one. They were to rule and reign from this place of unity, oneness, and balance.

When we build the concept of submission on that design, the picture is completely different than what we have been taught. Submission is more about *unity* than it is about who is in charge. From the faulty concept, submission is a solution to the *supposed* struggle for leadership. If we don't understand that men and women are equal counterparts, and instead we believe there is a fight for control, then submission means that women must give up, shut up, and stop fighting for the leadership role that wasn't theirs. Based on this error, there is only one winner and one loser, and the loser is womankind.

I have spoken with many married women over my years of women's ministry, and almost all the women I have spoken with have said the same thing. They have no desire to be in charge.

They want to follow. They want their man to be a leader. Many just want to be able to trust that their men truly love God and are listening to God. Most women just want to be heard, because it is the cry of our design. Our design says that we have internal perspectives and perceptions that are important and that need to be heard and validated. Men were not designed to lead alone, and deep down we all know that. We know that we are an important part of this team, and our opinions and perceptions are integral to solving the problems of our lives and our world. If our husbands truly understood our design, they would depend on us to supply our part. They need us as much as we need them. When men love the Lord and follow His leading, then it would be easy to follow. If men functioned from their original design and we functioned from ours, there wouldn't be demands, conflicts, and power struggles. There would be peace, ease, and mutual leadership.

This is the concept of true submission—or "mutual leadership"—that we see in Ephesians 5:21. Men and women were designed to submit to the strengths and position of the other. We were designed as one-flesh leadership team, each with their own position and function on this team, which infers we together submit, we each need to bring our part to the other. Woman should encompass man with her internal perspective and perceptions, and man should contain her with practical leadership and protection. The idea of mutual submission is much easier to understand when it's based on the way men and women were made to function. Do you see how differently God designed submission when you build from the truth about who we are? Submission is a way for us to stay in unity, to make better decisions as we rule and reign over His planet peacefully and powerfully. Submission is a powerful way to function together as two equal yet opposite, complementary parts of the same whole.

WHEN WOMEN ENCOMPASS

"In the same way [that Christ suffered], women, be submissive to your own husbands, that even if some do not obey the word, they, without a word, may be won over by the conduct of their wives."

—1 Peter 3:1-6, AMP

God's original plan was for women to live so close to His heart and spirit that we would be unoffended, unafraid, and unhindered from closeness with our men. As we encompassed them, we would pray for them and understand the issues in their hearts. We would know what God was doing and where He was working—everything for their good and our good. If we lived as God instructed, with Him as our Husband first, we would be able to win over our men without a word, because we would be flowing around them with the peaceful presence of God. How much easier and powerful is "submission" from this perspective? It is an entirely different picture.

In 2 Peter 3:7, after women are instructed to submit, men are reminded to dwell with us "with understanding, giving honor to the wife, as the weaker vessel *and* as being heirs *together* of the grace of life" (NKJV, emphasis added). This idea is exactly the picture that the Lord has revealed in our design. First of all, we *are* equal heirs. We function, *together*, as a two-part/one-flesh leadership team. The original design supports this idea of honoring women as the weaker vessel if we think of "weaker" as meaning "vulnerable," or "more sensitive." Yes, we are vulnerable, because woman was originally inside man's body! That is a real picture of vulnerable! Yes, we were made to be sensitive, and that is exactly why we should be *honored*; weaker doesn't mean "less than." Sensitivity is valuable and men need that from us. However, our sensitivity is also what makes us vulnerable. Think of a finely crafted instrument, such as a scientific instrument. The more delicate and precise the instrument, the "weaker" it is; it requires careful handling and protection, and moving an instrument like this requires much padding and a protective case; you can't be rough or careless with it. The more sensitive the instrument, the more delicate and easily damaged it is. Let's pretend that your health, your prosperity, your finances, and your very life depended on this sensitive instrument working properly. How carefully would you treat it? How much more carefully would you protect it? How much honor would you give it? If men understood that this is who women are to them, they would treat women much differently. If we understood this about ourselves, we would value ourselves more highly and speak more carefully. Men would welcome our opinions and perspectives, knowing that their very life may depend on them. Men would honor us when they understand that being "weaker" doesn't mean being "lesser" or "below" but being "finely honed" or "vulnerable yet powerful." Mutual submission is easy to understand when the true picture of who we are to each other is clear.

Christ is the head of the Church and the head of the man, and the man is the head of the woman. Man was the *literal* head in the original design; he had a physical head, and she didn't. How about that for literal interpretation? He was the physical, external manifestation of their union of one flesh. Men are still the head; that is not in question. It's just *how* they are the head that is significant. As we saw in chapter 2, science verifies that men are designed to think more practically and logically. They have a slight advantage in decision-making, but they were not designed to make decisions alone. They were designed to make decisions *with* us, to rule and reign *with* us. Does the Word say that men are to lead? Yes, but through a more equal balance of power, as they were designed as part of a two-part being. Women need men. We need their practical, black-and-white, compartmentalized way of thinking. It blends so well with ours. And men need us.

They need to hear our perspectives and our insights. We process information and are intelligent too; we just think *differently*. We supply men with a counterbalance of thought and perspective, which is critical for good decision-making. Our voices need to be heard, not just in decision-making but in all of life.

As Lisa Bevere says in her book *Lioness Arising*,

> "Men do not grow healthy and strong through the silence of women. Men grow healthy and strong by the addition of our voices because the challenge of a daughter's questions serves to raise men higher, which makes them freer. The perspective of women tempers and refines men, just as they create an environment for the women to flourish."

This is the beautiful and powerful picture of submission: thinking together, reasoning together, and honoring one another. Ruling and reigning from this place of mutual submission is productive, and it produces peaceful unity rather than a conflict-riddled power struggle. Men who are on fire for the Lord, men who are strong in character, and men who are willing to grow and love and build a marriage make our job as women who are called to submission much easier. However, many men are not there yet. In the meantime, we can still choose to be vessels that the Lord uses to touch the men and turn them back to their original position as leader, container, and protector. They *will* be our counterparts who rule, reign, multiply, and subdue the planet with us. They *will* honor us and value our voice, our perspective and all that we bring. They *will* live in *mutual submission* with us. God is restoring women in order to restore men, so *together* we can rule and reign with the authority, unity, creativity, and blessings intended for us. It's time to reclaim our power.

The Lord is after something big. He is setting the stage and is preparing His people for amazing and challenging days. *Society is built on families.* As women recapture their place and as men respond, families will be restored, and we will see great change in all of society.

"As the family goes, so goes the nation and so goes the whole world in which we live."

— Pope John Paul II

God has put in us the power to change our world. Let that truth come alive in you.

7
THE BIG PICTURE

> "The day will come when men will recognize woman as his peer, not only at the fireside, but in councils of the nation. Then, and not until then, will there be the perfect comradeship, the ideal union between the sexes that shall result in the highest development of the race."
> ‖ SUSAN B. ANTHONY

I love this quote by Susan B. Anthony because it is full of the hope that comes with prophetic vision. She saw the reconciliation between the sexes so long ago, and she knew that one day, the unity of men and women would result in a change in mankind—a more mature and evolved human race. Man will recognize woman as his peer, and woman will return to her powerful position. As we saw in the last chapter, the woman's position is a catalyst for change, change that is needed. As transformed and restored women increase in number and in their ability to encompass, we will see a corresponding shift in men, in marriages, in families, and, ultimately, in all aspects of culture and society. God wants to restore women and men, and He wants to restore marriages. He is after the holy union that He had in mind when He created mankind.

In the very beginning, immediately after God made mankind, He blessed them (see Genesis 1:28). In Hebrew, "blessed" is the word *barak*, which also means "to kneel."[40] I love this picture of our loving Father kneeling or bending down to bestow blessings on His creation. He blessed mankind with His favor, His presence, His glory, and all good things—just as He wants to do today. Where there is unity, God commands a blessing (see Psalm 133). We can recapture our original design of unity and the fullness of blessing that comes with it. His power and His glory and His presence can rest over and in every marriage. We *are* blessed when marriages function in unity as one flesh, and they release the power of God. As we function in oneness, we reflect the Lord and release His power and glory. We reflect His image even to the heavens; angels and archangels understand more of God as they see mankind reflecting His image (see Ephesians 3:10, 1 Peter 1:12). Everything came from Him. Then through the unity of man and woman, through His image and likeness, we steward His creation.

When men and women are reconciled and restored to our original design, the confusion of who we are and who we are to each other will disappear. The conflict and struggle in our relating will be gone. Struggle is the opposite of agreement, and when the struggle is gone, agreement is possible. Agreement is a building block of unity. Amos 3:3 says, "Can two walk together, except they be agreed?" (KJV). When we are restored, we act in tandem, in perfect order and unity. From that unity, a pathway is created for power to flow. When marriages are filled with power and authority, couples are able to fulfill their call to reign over this planet, multiplying and releasing the Kingdom. That was the plan from the very beginning: men and women working in tandem, influencing society by releasing the Kingdom, multiplying and reproducing, protecting all they reproduce, and subduing the forces of evil. Imagine if the full power of the Kingdom was in your marriage and in your home. We can recover this; it is the Lord's plan for us at this time. Can you imagine a society of restored men and women? Can you picture marriages that are blessed and full of the purpose, power, and unity seen in the Trinity? That is where this reconciliation is taking us. We could live to see the end of the oppression of women. The children of the world could be protected from the unspeakable horrors that many of them face every day. It all starts with men and women being restored to their original design.

Even though the marriage covenant relationship holds enormous power and a deeper opportunity for encompassing and influencing, it is not just the married women who can be catalysts for change. It is also powerful when single women are restored to their original design. Even if you never marry, you will likely interact with men—brothers or fathers or coworkers or friends—every day. As you embrace your original design and relate to men from your restored position, you too will effect change. Single moms, you can affect your relationships with your sons to be powerful and liberating for them and for you. God wants to restore all the men. There are lots of men around us—not just as husbands—and we can influence them every day. We still need what men bring to us, and they still need what we bring to them, single or married.

RELEASING THE FATHERS

The timing of the Lord is perfect. In Ecclesiastes 3:17, He says that He has a perfect and appointed time for all things. In Acts 3:21 He says that there will be a time when He will restore all things. Paul tells us in Ephesians 1:10, "And this is the plan: At the right time He will bring *everything* together under the authority of Christ—everything in heaven and on Earth" (NLT, emphasis added). We will see revival, reconciliation, and restoration of all things as He readies us for His return. It is not anything new to say that He is coming back soon and that revival will come before He returns. Most, if not all, of the major prophets of our time have released words about this end-time harvest that we are stepping into. It is abundantly clear that God is preparing all things for His return. One of the things He is preparing is His church. He is readying us for an end-time harvest. He is setting the stage for His return. He is preparing His people with the reconciliation of men and women to their restored original design as the two-part leadership team they were designed to be.

In Malachi 3, God said that He would send Elijah the prophet to us before the coming of the Lord and that He would restore the hearts of the fathers to their children and the hearts of the children to their fathers. Luke 1:17 echoes a similar message: "And he shall go before him in the spirit and power of Elijah, to turn the hearts of the fathers to the children, and the disobedient to the wisdom of the just—to make ready a people prepared for the Lord" (KJV). *This is the big picture.* When transformed women embrace their transformational God (see Jeremiah 31:22), they are filled to overflowing with His Spirit. From that overflow, they encompass their men. Then their men reclaim their place as containers, leaders, protectors, and fathers. It is in fatherhood that the original design of men is most apparent. Good fathers protect, lead and contain: they hold the family; they carry the family; they prevent the spread of evil; they are the containers.

As more and more women influence their men and create the space for them to step into as containers, marriages will function as holy unions—as one flesh in unity and power—and we will take back the planet. We are not just talking about taking back culture and society; we are taking back everything, restoring all things and releasing the fathers. This is how we will prepare the way for what God wants to do in these end times.

We learned that the word "encompass" also means to "turn back" or "turn around," and when we encompass men with God's Spirit, they are then free to "turn around" and "turn back" to their original place. Their orphan wounds are then healed as well, and they are restored to the heavenly Father. We encompass them with the Father and "turn them back" to Him. Then He, our perfect Father will release Himself in the men. Women release the Father *around* men, and He releases the Father *in* men. This release of the Father will turn men around, and the Malachi word can be fulfilled. Our Father God is released and the fathers are released.

We are at the most exciting time in history. Are there dark times ahead? Yes. Is evil increasing on the planet? Yes. However, we can be excited because we are also going to see an increased release of our *Abba*, Daddy God and our earthly dads! When life is full of risk and danger, it's our Daddy we need. When children are afraid of the "big bad guys," they generally run to their dads. What do fathers do? Fathers release courage and identity and strength. Fathers protect and provide. That's what we need today. In these challenging end times, we need our Father and the fathers on this planet to protect, provide, and lead us. The world is crying out for fathers to take their place. The Earth is crying out for the release of the Father and the fathers on this planet. The intensity of the battle has increased because the stage is being set for His return. The children need their dads, earthly and heavenly.

We need dads who will fight for us! Interesting to note that the Hebrew word used for "man" in the Jeremiah passage is *geber* (H1397), which means "warrior."[41] That passage can read "a woman will encompass a *warrior*" not just a man. It was God's desire for women to encompass *warriors*, men who can be restored and function as warriors; we are surrounding the warriors with the Spirit of God. This is probably my favorite part of this verse, the reality that our men will be the warriors we want them to be! What woman doesn't love a warrior? What woman isn't stirred by the warriors we see in movies or read about in books? Russell Crowe as General Maximus in *Gladiator*, or Mel Gibson as Sir William Wallace in *Braveheart*, Aragon in the *Lord of the Rings* trilogy, men who bravely fight for their women and their people. What woman doesn't want to be fought for? We all do because we were built that way! We were designed to be in partnership with men who are warriors! We are to encompass our warriors who *will* fight for us (and with us right by their side as their *ezer kennegdo*) because that's what warriors do. Call out the warrior in your men, speak to the warrior in him, and pray for the warrior to be released. Can you imagine a society filled with warrior-fathers?

GOD'S ATTENTION IS ON WOMEN

As He is setting the stage, His *attention* is on women, but His *intention* is for men.

Let me explain. Women are the way to the Lord's goal to release men to fatherhood. He knows how He made us. We were designed to influence as we encompass. He knows that we are the "source of life" that men need. He knows women are the *ezer kennegdo*. *We were designed to bring the warrior men our strength of a deep and intimate heart without fear or need.* We were designed with the strength of our voice that challenges and encourages. We are meant to carry the Lord to men and around their hearts. God wants to work with us so we help Him touch the hearts of men, of warriors, and turn them back to the children. Our first step, as women, is to respond to His call. He is calling to us, and we need to respond with "YES!"

For those of you complaining, "Why us? Why can't the men change first?" let me give you two reasons why healing and restoration start with us. First, because it is our design. Remember, the relationship between men and women has a flow that begins

THE BIG PICTURE

with the women. We encompass them, and they respond. We create atmosphere in and around our men and families. We start the flow, and men respond back; this is who He made us to be. The most effective way to change men is to start with us and let the men respond, as they were designed to. (Remember, that was the very dynamic that even the Enemy exploited to get to the heart of mankind.) Second, God is beginning with us because we are responsible for the dynamic of the relationship. We changed the dynamic in the garden when we brought death instead of life. We started the flow of sin that created the corrupt design. (To be clear: man is also culpable. He accepted the death with which he was encompassed, so he carries the responsibility of releasing sin and death energy. What will happen as that is reversed and healed? I don't know, but I can't wait to find out! That is another book for someone else to write.) For now, we know that God wants our design to be restored so He can touch the hearts of men through us. This happens as we accept the responsibility to bring change to the relationship. We started the corrupt dynamic, and it is our responsibility and, more importantly, our *design* to influence, to encompass, to turn them around and turn them back and begin the transformation back to the original design. This is why His attention is on us. We are needed.

It is clear that the Lord planned since the very beginning to work through women to bring this restoration and reconciliation. Look back for a moment to Genesis 3:15; it shows us the Lord's plan. In it, God says that the woman will crush the head of Satan. A deep-seated hatred exists between the Enemy and us, but we *will* get the victory. Women *will* crush the enemy. We *will* get the victory *when we encompass men with life*. Again, Jeremiah 31:22 says, "For the Lord has created a new thing: a woman shall encompass a man" (KJV). In this passage, the word "new" doesn't translate as a brand-new thing but rather as a *restored* thing. He is restoring, reconciling, and bringing men and women back together. God is saying that we women will be *restored* back to our original design to encompass and surround our men with His Spirit. When we are restored, men are restored, and our unity releases the Kingdom and crushes the head of the Enemy. The Enemy will no longer be able to work through men to oppress us, silence us, and hurt us. He will not be able to use us to encompass men with our need, our emptiness. God had planned from the beginning that one day He would work through women as He restores us back to our position and bring the victory.

What has been hidden until the appointed time is now being revealed. The Lord has decided that this is the time to make *us* aware of how He made us, who He made us to be, and the power that we hold as women. It is time for us to understand our value and our responsibility to men. God wants us to know how we were designed, because He wants us to work with Him to reach men and to call forth the warrior-fathers. This is His strategy—women influencing men—and He has used this same strategy before.

God has worked through women to influence men many times. While Jesus was on this planet, every major truth revealed about Him was either first told *to* women or was proclaimed *through* women. Jesus was not the earthly king that many expected, nor was He only a prophet as some suspected; He was ushering in the heavenly Kingdom on Earth. He, the King of kings, was going to die on the cross so they could live! He was the Messiah bringing a new covenant to Earth! As He fulfilled His purpose and prepared His people for what was to come, oftentimes He needed to get past their mental reasoning and expectations and reveal to their spirits the truth, truth about who *He* was and what *His* purpose was. These were not easy concepts to grasp. They weren't to be understood with the intellect, but with the heart and spirit. The best way for God to reach the hearts of His people was to go to the one who was designed to live next to mankind's heart: woman. This domain of revelation and spirit is where women were designed to function best! He went to women first with each major revelation. (The fact that He went to women first should be enough to stop every man who says that women should be silent in church!) Jesus did not expect silence from women. On the contrary, He worked through our design and told us to proclaim truth!

WOMEN PROCLAIMING TRUTH

Every major truth about Jesus went to or through women. For example, He chose to be born into this planet as a human baby, *through* the body of a woman. He could have chosen another way to come to our realm, but He chose to be born as a human. He chose one of His precious women, Mary, and He also first revealed to her that she was carrying the Lord. He didn't tell a man. He didn't tell her fiancé, Joseph first, nor did He tell Mary's earthly father. Then, He revealed the Lordship of Jesus to Elizabeth. He did not tell her husband, the priest; He told Elizabeth. Look at the passage in Luke 1:39-56; we see that when Mary went to visit Elizabeth, Elizabeth asked, "How is it that the mother of my Lord should come to visit me?" She had had a revelation that the baby in Mary's womb is the Lord. At that time, the Bible only records these two women as being aware that the King, the Lord, was growing in Mary's womb. Two *women* were the first to know. After Christ was born, God chose another woman, the prophetess Anna, to publicly declare that the baby Jesus was the Savior. This was the way the Father God chose to bring His Son into the Earth realm—as a baby grown in the womb of a woman and His Lordship proclaimed by women.

Jesus also chose a woman to announce and confirm His coming death. In Luke 7:43, a woman anoints Jesus' feet with oil at a dinner party. Jesus alludes to her having been led by the Spirit to anoint Him. Her decision to come to the dinner was bold, but Jesus does not scorn her or look down on her. Instead, He justifies and validates her action. He reveals that she is doing what needs to be done to prepare Him for His death. This is powerful revelation and a teaching moment for the men. Most certainly, some of these men were not expecting Jesus to die; they were looking for deliverance from Roman rule, hoping that Jesus was their answer. Pay close attention to what is recorded in this passage. It says that Jesus *looks at* the woman anointing Him but *speaks to* Simon. Was this His goal? To speak to the men through the actions of this woman? I believe so. Like today, *His attention is on us but His intention is for the men.*

A woman is also the first to know that Jesus was Christ, the Messiah. He chose a Samaritan woman at a well—a woman who had had several husbands and several men in her life—to reveal this truth to (see John 4:4–42). In the long dialogue between them, He reveals to her that it is through Him that we receive eternal life (see 4:13–14), that He desires to love all people (see 4:7–9), and most amazingly, that He is the Messiah. "The woman said, 'I know that Messiah (called Christ) is coming. When He comes, He will explain everything' to us. Jesus answered, 'I who speak to you am He'" (John 4:25–26, NIV). Incredible revelation that no one else has yet heard, she is the first to know. She, a woman, is the first to learn from Jesus Himself the most amazing truth: He is the Messiah! What happens next is important for us, too. It is where we are today: "The woman then left her water pot, and went her way into the city, *and said to the men...*" (John 4:28, emphasis added). She leaves her water pot because she now has found the living water, and she goes back to her village and proclaims *to the men* the good news that she has found the Messiah. I find this amazing that a woman is the first to receive the revelation that Christ is the Messiah, and she goes to proclaim this truth *to the men*. Her influence causes the village to receive Jesus, too. She encompasses her village with truth, and the people are changed. The men respond.

Just as Christ worked through this woman at the well, He wants to work through us. We were designed to live in the spirit realm and to be intimate with our God. We were designed to influence men. God wants to partner with us today in the same way He worked through the women of the Bible. We have a voice, and it is time to be heard.

The amazing revelation of His resurrection was also first given to women. Reporting on Jesus on the cross, Matthew 27:55 says, "And many women were there looking on from a distance, who had followed Jesus from Galilee, ministering to Him." Here we see women watching it all unfold and ministering to Him however they can. I assume that means they were praying for Him, crying for Him, and trying to alleviate some of His emotional anguish and pain. After He died, His body was taken from the cross. Joseph of Arimathea took His body and put Him in a tomb. Verse 61 says, "Mary Magdalene and the other Mary were sitting there opposite the tomb" (NIV). The women watched where Joseph took Christ's body and stayed there, caring for and about Jesus. The next thing we see in the morning after the Sabbath, at the very break of day, is the return of the women: "Now, after the Sabbath, as it began to dawn toward the first day of the week, Mary Magdalene and the other Mary came to look at the grave, and behold a severe Earthquake had occurred, for an angel of the Lord descended from heaven and came and rolled away the stone and sat upon it" (Matthew 28:1). These women had been literally following Jesus for days. As women were designed to do, they came close to Him, close to His heart with their hearts, and were willing to carry pain and heartbreak in the midst of confusion. It must have been frightening for the women to see that Jesus' body was gone, but the angel told them, "Do not be afraid: for I know that you are looking for Jesus who has been crucified. He is not here, for He has risen, just as He said" (28:5). Although some men were there standing guard, the angel spoke *to the women*. They were the first to hear. After times of fear, confusion, and grief, the greatest truth in all history is revealed to these women: He lives. He is not dead! The women receive this truth! Then, the angel tells them, "Go quickly and *tell His disciples* that He is risen from the dead; and behold, He is going before you into Galilee, there you will see Him; behold, I have told you. And they departed quickly from the tomb with fear and great joy and ran to report it to His disciples" (28:7–8, ASV, emphasis added). After they are told the good news, the women are sent to tell the disciples; they are sent *to tell the men*. His attention is on us but his *intention* is for the men!

This is where we are today. Just as the Lord has worked through women in the past to reach men with truth and to encompass them with His Spirit, the Lord wants to work through women today to reach men. He knows we can because that is how He made us, as powerful influencers. We are being restored to our God-given abilities to encompass, to influence, and to flow His Spirit around them; now we will encompass with the Spirit of God in a circuit of life energy. No longer will we be slaves to corruption and encompass with our "intense craving" full of need; now we can encompass with life. We *can* influence men. We *can* be a source of life that God uses to turn them back and turn them around. We were designed to.

This ability and our design are what the Enemy exploited in the garden. The Enemy also knows how we were designed and that we can influence men. Starting with Eve, the Enemy has many times worked through women to defeat men, knowing their powerful ability to influence. Sampson lost his position because of Delilah, who manipulated him with her womanly abilities into revealing his source of power and strength. Solomon was undone by his foreign wives who influenced him to worship their foreign gods. Ahab was brought down by the powerful influence of Jezebel, as she influenced him and the entire kingdom toward idolatry. The Enemy knows the power of our design, and he exploits our corrupted pattern to keep us from the Lord and focused on men and our intense craving. He uses us to encompass men with our need and our brokenness, encompassing them with sin and death. Since the beginning of time, the Enemy has known of women's power to influence men. However, the really good news is that God knows too, and now, so do we!

It is time to crush the Enemy's head. We are now surrendering our mirrors, holding onto God, and encompassing men with life. We will influence them with life and love and will release our men to their places as containers, leaders, warriors and fathers. In this, women will crush the Enemy.

The question now is to you. Are you willing to say yes to the call? To accept your position? Are you willing to receive the Lord as your Savior, your Father, and your Husband, and to cling to Him first? Let His powerful love fill you to overflowing. Are you willing to be satisfied in His love and to let Him meet all your needs? Are you willing to let go of expectations and offenses and any unforgiveness toward men and let Him heal your wounds? I know many of you have been wounded, but it is time to let go. Will you let Him restore your voice? Will you let Him restore your true power? Will you let Him protect you, defend you, honor you, and bring you into your full womanhood? Will you let go of your mirror, your self, and exchange it for His mirror to lose yourself in His glory? Will you live this way every day to the best of your ability, trusting Him to give you the strength? Will you step into your place as an encompasser and trust God with the results? Will you settle into His timing and path to bring about change in you and the men in your world? Will you let Him be in control? Will you release your husband or your future husband into God's hands and then leave him there? Will you trust God to work in men in your life the way He has promised?

I know this isn't easy, and I am not asking you to do something that I am not willing to do. This process has not always gone the way I expected or wanted. It has been full of sacrifice and painful moments and tears, but it has also been full of Him, of joy, freedom, and peace. I would not have any other life but the life He has called me to, and I'm honored to be part of what He is releasing on the planet. I pray that you are willing, too. I pray you say yes to God and join me in the call to recapture our true position as women. I pray you join this great movement of God.

THE NEW WOMEN'S MOVEMENT

Matthew Arnold, a nineteenth-century British poet and author, said, "If ever comes a time when the women of the world come together purely and simply for the benefit of mankind, it will be a force such as the world has never known." This is the New Women's Movement. This book is a call to bring together an end-time army of women to assemble together, to surrender to the Lord, to be freed from our corrupted design, and to encompass, encircle, and surround the hearts of men. Together we will watch our men take their rightful place and join with us to release our Father and His Kingdom.

As the Lord spoke to me about bringing together this army of women who will touch the hearts of men, He took me back to the Exodus 38:8 scripture: "And he made the laver of brass, and the foot of it of brass, of the looking glasses of the women assembling, which assembled at the door of the tabernacle of the congregation" (KJV). He had me first look at the word "assembled"; in Hebrew it means "come together as an army." These women came together like an army. And who were they? They were women who were serving the Lord, as near to the presence of the Lord as they could be in that culture. They were passionate lovers of God and assembled together to worship and serve Him. They were joined together as an *army*.

And again, what did this army of women do? They surrendered their mirrors. They gave up their precious mirrors into a blazing hot fire and instead created something to purify their men. They gave up their ability to even see themselves so that the men could. What an incredible sacrifice! The women's sacrificial mirrors were melted into a bronze laver to cleanse men so they could stand before the Lord as clean *and* in their rightful place. As we surrender to Him our mirrors, our very selves, we get His glory. From that He creates something that cleanses our men and gives them purified hearts so they're able to take their rightful place, too. This is a truth worth meditating on.

This picture of united women, encouraging and supporting each other to surrender their lives to the perfect loving Savior, Father, and Husband, is so exciting to me. I can see this group of beautiful women worshiping the King. The King of the universe who loves on us outrageously. We are meant to be His beautiful, loved army of princess warriors. I can also see the men as pure, holy, and standing in their place as the containers, leaders, and protectors of women and of all mankind, our warrior partners. Fathers' hearts are being released. Behind them are children who are protected, safe, pure, innocent, and growing in the glorious presence of our good, good Father and King.

AN ARMY OF WOMEN

Psalm 68:11 says, "The Lord announces the word, and the women who proclaim it are a mighty throng" (NIV). We are a might throng and we will proclaim His word! This is the New Women's Movement and here is our strategy:

1
WE ARE TRANSFORMED WOMEN.

Jeremiah 31:22 is more than the founding scripture that reveals our call to encompass the hearts of men. In *The Message* translation, the same scripture says, "A transformed woman will embrace her transforming God." We begin by becoming transformed women, restored to our rightful position and free from the corrupt design. A transformed woman can live in the Kingdom in close relationship with God—not "needing" a man but filled with the Lord and in right relationship with men. Transformed women have disengaged their hearts from the "I need a man" craving and have had their hearts healed by the love of our Father.

Transformed women embrace their God. They have surrendered all of themselves to Him, as passionate lovers. He is their everything. He is their Savior, their Father, and their Husband. They have surrendered their mirror and exchanged it for His glory. They live a life for Him and no longer live for "me, me, me." They daily choose Him over themselves. This is the surrendered life.

THE BIG PICTURE

When we choose to be women who are on fire for our Lord and King, we have access to the throne, the very presence of our Lord. We are not forced to stay outside and in the doorway like the women of the past. We are able to lose ourselves in His presence, which is where we find ourselves. We release the Holy Spirit that is already inside us, and we can daily live in our true and rightful position as women.

2
WE WILL BE AN ARMY OF WOMEN ASSEMBLED IN UNITY.

The next step is to help other women be transformed too. Elizabeth Blackwell, the first woman to become a physician in the US, said, "For what is done or learned by one class of women becomes, by virtue of their common womanhood, the property of all women."

Being in unity with other women will require healing. Many of us will need help and support as we reclaim our lost design and walk with God in the role of encompasser. Some women have difficult marriages and deep wounds to work through. We need the support of our sisters. Unfortunately, some women have been hurt by other women, which will make it harder for them to join in. We have betrayed, excluded, gossiped, judged, competed with, and stolen one another's men and friends often enough that many women don't even want to think about turning to another woman for support. I hear that from women every day, and I understand. The story about the woman at the well will help us. She was drawing water at a time when she knew other women wouldn't be there. She was hiding from women — probably women who had hurt her, judged her, and criticized her. Yet she later carried the message of the Messiah to them and brought to them salvation. We have all been hurt, and we can understand why the woman wanted to hide; we can identify with the woman at the well. However, if we can remember just one time when we treated another woman poorly, we are also the women of the village. Have we not all, at least once, gossiped, excluded, judged, or betrayed another woman? We are both the wounded and the wounder. If we start by acknowledging this truth, we can heal. Every woman has been hurt by and has hurt another woman. We are not alone; we are in this together.

Proverbs says that we are not to hide ourselves from our own flesh. In this case, flesh means "gender." When you hide from other women, you also hide your needed gifts from them. The woman at the well was an anointed evangelist, but no one knew that until she let God be her everything. He quenched her thirst for love, and then she went back to her town and turned them all to God. Some women who had previously hurt her were saved because of her gift of evangelism. And their husbands and their children were also saved. This all happened because the woman at the well stopped hiding. She was set free, and she used her gift to serve the very people who had hurt her.

When one of us hides, all of us suffer. Let go of offense; forgive and take hold of your sisters in the Lord and bring your gifts to them. You are needed. Reach out to other women again ask the Lord to help you find women who are safe. We cannot restore our lives, our men, our families, and our communities without each other. We need every gift and every heart of strength. We must be united. Be willing to let God heal your heart from the offenses of other women, and choose to be united.

Some of you have difficult situations, wounds from your childhood, messy marriages, and hurting children. Some of you will not be able to go forward without help—especially the help of your big sisters who have gone before you. They can support you as you open your heart to God, recapture your original design, find your voice and use it, and be the influencer and encompasser of your home. Some of you single women have run from man to man for many years. Some of you have put your life on hold, waiting for a man to show up. Some of you have held on to resentments toward men or about being single for many years. To break these patterns, you will need to face your loneliness and pain, and you will need the support of another woman who understands this pain and the process of healing. We are the army, and we need each other's prayers and support. We need to walk alongside each other as we grow. Let go of any offenses you carry from other women. Let God heal your wounds, and reach out to each other in support.

Make a commitment toward other women to not betray or gossip or intentionally hurt them in any way. And also commit that if anyone hurts you, you will not stay offended and hide. There is nothing that destroys an army more effectively than when that army fights itself from within, crumbling from the inside. Which is why we need to make these commitments toward unity and strong relationships and to stay away from offenses. Make this your new way of living.

3
WE WILL ENCOMPASS OUR MEN AND ALLOW THE WOUNDS WE'VE RECEIVED FROM MEN TO BE HEALED.

Together as an army, we are meant to fight for and with our husbands (current or future), our brothers, our sons, our fathers, our pastors, our friends, and for all the men of our world. We do this in intercession, in relationship, and in declaration, and our power flows from our transformed hearts. We encompass our men with the power of the Lord and with the support of the other members of our army.

Understand and embrace that encompassing a man may look a little different from woman to woman and from season to season. There are seasons of fierce intercession, and there are seasons in which we need to worship and rest and allow the Lord to fight for us. There are seasons in which He asks us to use the voice He has given us to speak words of truth that may be challenging. Then there are other seasons in which we are silent—encompassing men with our private prayers and quiet actions rather than our words. There are seasons of setting firm boundaries and establishing order, and there are open seasons, free from restraint. In all these seasons, how we encompass may look slightly different from one woman to another. As long as we stay connected to the Lord and hear His direction, we will know what to do and how to encompass. We will hear and obey. He is the good Shepherd, and He will lead us. He promises that we will hear His voice (see John 10:27). Our relationship with Him is the foundation from which we can reach out to encompass our men.

Many of you have deep wounds from abuses that you have suffered at the hands of a man. Maybe you've been hurt by an uncle or a brother or even your father or your husband. The idea of encompassing a man is probably a bit frightening or offensive to you. Yet this is the path, as painful as it is. The Lord wants to heal you, too. Letting go is the key to moving forward. Being fully who you were designed to be as a woman will bring great healing to you. Some of you may need professional help as you uncover some of your wounds, and my prayer is that you would do whatever it takes to heal. Ask the Lord for healing, and He will provide it.

4
WE WILL RESTORE AND RECAPTURE OUR FAMILIES.

As an army of transformed women, we will bring transformation to our marriages and families. We will work with the Holy Spirit, and some of us will work with our husbands, to restore our homes to unity, peace, and order. We will bring the King and the Kingdom into our homes and families in increasing measure. From that place of strength, we will march on. As each marriage returns to the original design, and as husband and wife function as one flesh, we will march on. As marriages function from this restored place, we will march on in authority and power. The original design is one of agreement. Where there is agreement, there is unity, and where there is unity, there is power. We will bring that power to our families, and we will take authority over the Enemy and all he has tried to destroy.

A successful army needs a good defense as well as a strong offense. Having a good defense requires protecting your vulnerabilities. If we are to be a strong force of women, we need to protect our homes and families; they cannot be exposed and vulnerable. We cannot be a strong force when our own households are a mess. The word "encompass" can mean to "turn around," and we can trust that as we encompass, we will see even the most difficult situations turn around. Even the messiest of situations can change and every marriage and every family can become healthy. Having a strong family and/or a strong marriage is the best defense. When you function from your original design and when your family is in order, your family will be protected and your vulnerabilities will be lessened. When you and your family have a good foundation, you will be able to fight freely. You will be able to join the offense to fight for, come alongside of, and build other women. A good defense rests on the power of a unified army and a solid foundation.

When women and men function in their original design, marriages are restored. Restored marriages flourish and function in God's original design of one flesh. They reflect the image of God, of the Trinity. The Trinity is in a sense a "family" that functions in complete order and unity. That is what God wants to establish in us. Can you imagine society full of restored marriages—full of the purpose, power, and unity that is seen in the Trinity? We were designed to function in that same unity. As men and women function in the original design of one flesh and as they are connected to the Spirit of God, they reflect the Lord and release Him, His Kingdom, His power, and His glory. When we are united with God and with each other (having right relationship with other women), and when we have solid foundations in our marriages and families, God can be released in the world through us.

"If there is righteousness in the heart, there will be beauty in the character. If there is beauty in the character, there will be harmony in the home. If there is harmony in the home, there will be order in the nations. When there is order in the nations, there will peace in the world."

—Confucious

If we choose to, we can change the world.

God might say to us today, "I know that since the Fall, you have had conflict-filled relationships with men. Your hurt and loss have driven you to chase them, only to be oppressed, abandoned, and broken-hearted. But I will return you to your true place. Your place of power was stolen from you by the Enemy. He has used your corrupted design to batter you and oppress you and hold you down, but you—My beautiful, powerful daughters—are going to crush his head. You are the victors. Since the beginning, I knew that there would be a day when I would reverse these consequences and would return you to your place of power. That day has come, and you are My weapons to crush the Enemy, to bring healing to men, and to begin the release of My Fatherhood to this orphaned world."

This is His new movement, and it brings a new wave of His anointing. He is holding out His hand, beckoning you to join Him. See His eyes, filled with the love that will restore you. Hear His voice as He sings to you, His beloved, His fair one: "Come away with Me on this journey, and find peace and joy and freedom."

Won't you please join Him?

ONE LAST WORD
FOR THE MEN

I assume that mostly women will read this book, yet I think it is important to address some things to the men who may be reading this. First of all, congratulations! I hope all men read this book, because it is the key to what the Lord wants to do in our world at this time. He wants to restore women, and He also also wants to restore you and bring you together to release power. He wants to bring men back to their right place and stir up the fathers to release revival in the next generation. One of the ways He will touch you is through your wife or through women. He is restoring His original design in her, which will cause her to relate with you the way she was designed to. She was created and designed to influence you, surround you, and release the Spirit of God over you and your marriage. It is a full circle: women are transformed, and then the power to influence draws you into more of who God made you to be. God wants to release the power of manhood—and more specifically fatherhood—and He is beginning this transformation by restoring womanhood. I believe that there is much more to understand about how we were originally created, and I expect the Lord will continue to reveal more and more. I look forward to the Lord showing us more details about the original design of men. For now, I would like to share some of what He has shown me about men.

Jeremiah 31:22 says, "Behold I will do a new thing, a woman will encompass a man" (NIV). Through this scripture, God showed me His plan to restore women back to our original design. The interesting thing in this scripture is that the word for "man" isn't the gendered term for "male"; instead, the word really means "warrior." Woman was made to encompass you as your *ezer kennegdo*, which means the one who will fight by your side as your opposite and corresponding strength. So the Lord is saying to His warriors (men) that He will restore your woman to fight by your side, *with* you and not *against* you. I bet this is good news to some of you who have felt like you've had a war in your home. This is a new way of life for you and for her, and it ends with warrior men and their warrior princess brides ruling the planet, fighting together (not fighting each other).

Just as the key for the restoration of *women* is a close relationship with the Lord as her Savior, Father, and Husband, a close relationship with the Lord is key for *you*, too. Chapter 5 explains how to step into this life. Please be certain that you have surrendered your own life and are willing to do whatever the Lord asks you to do. Choose to be unoffended and to forgive your wife. Until she is healed, she is bound to the corrupt dynamic that makes her unable to freely relate with you. Gloria Steinem once said, "The problem for all of us, men and women, is not to learn, but to unlearn." Be open to learning new things about your wife's true position and yours. Ask the Lord to show you what His original intentions are for you as a man. Be the warrior.

The Lord made it clear to me that men were created to be women's *containers*, as protectors, and as leaders. You house us. You hold us. You protect us—sometimes even from our own selves. As the Bible says, women are the weaker sex, as in more *vulnerable*, in the context of how sensitively we function and discern. We need you to protect us in that, especially, because we sense things all the time. We need you to listen to our perspectives with an open heart and an open mind and to *then* take everything to the Lord.

What women bring you is powerful. It could be full of life or death, or full of her needs and hurts. You need to find out from the Lord what it is. She may be bringing to you something that will support actual life—you or your children or your business may depend on it. Adam accepted the death energy that Eve brought to him without questioning it, and he was held responsible for bringing death to the planet. Adam, not Eve, was responsible for releasing death. If he had contained her, as he was designed to do, and lead her properly, he could have stopped the flow of death. Instead, he received it and released it. You are the leader, the container, and the protector. This is a huge responsibility and your wife can share that pressure.

Your wife's insights and opinions matter. She was designed to supply you with needed balance. Honor and value that. It is your job to listen to her and to not shut her down. Do not ignore her intuition—especially when she has a feeling about something and has no logical reason for feeling that way. Listen and pray. Is this the Lord speaking through her? Many times it is. Value and consider her insights, and learn how to make decisions with her, prayerfully. Her opinions and yours will work to create solutions and direction. Adam and Eve worked as one and functioned in unity and power. Your wife is your *ezer kennegdo*—your opposite and complementary strength. She supplies something you are missing. Many times she thinks with her heart, and she has a viewpoint and a perspective that are different than yours. Listen and prayerfully apply her perspective to what God has shown you. Don't ignore her, but don't be passive and agree with everything she says either; that is what Adam did, and he brought death to the world. Rise up to your place as a container, protector, and leader of mankind.

Resist the pull of the corrupted design. Don't overpower your wife or push her away. Don't withdraw, as much as it feels like you need to. Resist the urge to rule over her; the power of that corrupted position is real. As your wife reassumes her position, you will be released to function more and more like your original design. Remember that woman caused the corrupted relationship pattern, and you received it by default. She can change it, she and the Lord, and her power to influence you in a new way will release a new relationship pattern for both of you. However, it is a process. In that process, you can help her and help yourself. Understand and encourage her to be who she was created to be, and that will free you. No matter what she chooses, you can still decide to move away from your corrupted design and seek freedom. The original design for both of you is a place of power.

Malachi 2:13–15 says, "But did He not make them one, Having a remnant of the Spirit? And why one? He seeks godly offspring. Therefore take heed to your spirit, And let none deal treacherously with the wife of his youth" (NKJV). Woman was designed to live inside you. She is truly your own flesh, which is why the Lord says to love her as you do your own flesh (see Ephesians 5:28). This is literal as well as figurative. Love her as Christ loves the Church, and cherish her. That is a huge job, but the Lord will help you. I believe the more you grow in your understanding of your relationship, the easier it will be to cherish her. As she grows in her ability to be who God called her to be, she will make mistakes. However, you are still to love her, as she is your flesh. That is a truth worth meditating on.

Ephesians 5:26 tells you to present your wife to the Lord and to wash her with the Word. Pray for her. Ask the Lord to restore her to who He created her to be. Ask the Lord to be her Husband, her Father, and her Savior. This is part of your position: to follow the Lord's example. Christ says He will present His Bride one day without spot or blemish; His Bride will be without fault and holy. How about your wife? Do you present her as faultless? Or do you, like Adam, blame her for everything and function like a fallen man? One definition of "contain" is "to prevent the spread of something." Part of your job as container is to prevent the spread of sin, evil, and death over your wife and you and your family. You are to preserve her. You are to preserve your children. Go before the Lord and pray for your family. Present your wife as blameless, and ask the Lord to make her whole and holy, which will protect your children as well.

This is the original dynamic: in her perfect design, your wife must be first married to the Lord. From that relationship, she can then flow around you. She is to stay filled with the Lord and walking in the Spirit continually; then your job is to love, cherish, and protect her. Are you encouraging her to follow the Lord? Have you released her to put the Lord ahead of you? In her corrupted position, you are the idol she looks to. It might be satisfying to you in some way for a woman to need you that much and want you that deeply. But it can also be overwhelming and draining. In any case, you must release her. Let her fall in love with the Lord, and let her love the Lord more than you. Speak the Word over her, and remind her that the Lord will meet her every need.

Women need to be loved and cherished and made to feel safe and secure—as well as many other emotional needs. Proverbs 30:23 says the Earth cannot bear up under an unloved woman when she is married. Why? When a woman is married, she brings to the table her enormous unmet needs and expects man to fill them. If she has not been loved by parents, grandparents or a parental figure, or if she has not allowed God to love her in the deepest parts of her being, she is unloved. An unloved woman is helpless against the corrupt dynamic. She will encompass you from the corrupt pattern she inherited from Eve and will expect, demand or manipulate you to fill her heart. When she is controlled by her unloved heart, she will try all sorts of tactics to get you to prove your love. An unloved woman can be distant, angry, depressed, manipulative, critical, needy, demanding, or resentful. Acknowledge to her and to yourself that you cannot fully meet her needs. *You cannot fill her 100 percent but you can give 100 percent of yourself.* Accept that. Step to the side when you need to, and make room for the Lord to love her first. You are not responsible or able to meet her needs *completely*, but you are still called to love and cherish with all that you have.

If you are only willing to do one thing, daily ask the Lord to meet your wife's need for love. If you are willing to do two things, then be a willing vessel for Him to love her through, too.

John Eldredge says in *Captivating*:

What is this thing in me—and in most men—that just doesn't want to go deep into a woman's world? "You are too much. Too hard. It's too much work. Men are simpler. Easier."... Now, part of a man's fundamental reluctance to dive into the world of a woman comes from a man's deepest fear, failure...He fears that having delved into his woman's world, he won't have what it takes to help her there. That's his sin, his cowardice. And because of her shame, most of the time a man gets away with it. Most marriages (and long term dating relationships) reach this sort of unspoken settlement. "I'm not coming any closer. This is as far as I am willing to go. But I won't leave, and that ought to make you happy."

Please, men, resist the corrupt dynamic and go forward. You do have what it takes; God already gave it to you!

A WORD TO THE SINGLE MEN

Single men who want to marry can start here too. Get comfortable with intimacy. Learn the skills and find the courage. Get ready to be the container and leader, which requires an intimate connection to the one who will internally influence you. Prepare yourself, but also be careful how and who you choose. The most important thing to look for in a future wife is a *loved woman* (see Proverbs 30:23). She may have been loved as a child by her parents, grandparents or parental figures, but you know for sure that she is loved when she knows her Savior, her loving Father, and her perfect Husband, and is settled in those relationships. Intimacy with a loved woman is a completely different experience than with an unloved woman. A loved woman can actually love you! If she has not been loved and if she does not have a deep and meaningful connection with the Lord, the perfect Father, then she is an "unloved woman." If she is an unloved woman, she is still a slave to the corrupt design pattern she inherited. She has not resolved the unmet emotional needs of an unloved orphan; she is desperate for attention, affection, and provision. *You cannot bear up under that*. The Lord has told you in Proverbs that the *Earth itself* cannot bear up under that, so you have been warned! If you engage in relationship with her, you will be drawn into the corrupt dynamic, and you will repeat Adam's pattern. You will want to rule over her by oppressing her or by withdrawing from her, and you will end up feeling like a failure. You are powerless to completely fill her needs; in some deep place, you probably know that already. Look for a woman who is loved and be thankful that you understand this very important truth. In the meantime, grow in God and become the warrior God has called you to be. He will bring you your warrior bride.

NOTES

1. George Carlin. *Men are from Earth, women are from Earth. Deal...* (n.d.). http://www.goodreads.com/quotes/33746-men-are-from-Earth-women-are-from-Earth-deal-with

2. Matthew Henry. *Matthew Henry's Commentary on the Whole Bible.* (n.d.). https://www.goodreads.com/author/quotes/91281.Matthew_Henry

3. Strong, J., & Strong, J. (1984). *The New Strong's Exhaustive Concordance of the Bible*: With main concordance, appendix to the main concordance, key verse comparison chart, dictionary of the Hebrew Bible, dictionary of the Greek Testament. Nashville: Thomas Nelson Publishers.

4. *The Names & Attributes of God.* El Shaddai. (n.d.). http://www.myredeemerlives.com/namesofgod/el-shaddai.html

5. Goldin, S. (2007). *Unlocking the Torah Text: An In-depth Journey into the Weekly Parsha: Bereishit.* New York: Jerusalem.

6. *Not Good for Man to Be Alone* - OU Torah. (n.d.). https://www.ou.org/torah/parsha/rabbi-goldin-on-parsha/not_good_for_man_to_be_alone

7. *What's the Truth about... Adam's Spare Rib?* - Jewish Action. (n.d.). https://www.ou.org/jewish_action/12/2007/whats_the_truth_about_adams_spare_rib/

8. Moen, S. (2011, May 22). *The Bloods of Your Brother | Hebrew Word Study | Skip Moen.* http://skipmoen.com/2011/05/the-bloods-of-your-brother/

9. Richoka. Messianic-revolution.com/2-20-hebrew-word-for-life-shows-evolution-is-wrong

10. Strong, J., & Strong, J. (1984). *The New Strong's Exhaustive Concordance of the Bible*: With main concordance, appendix to the main concordance, key verse comparison chart, dictionary of the Hebrew Bible, dictionary of the Greek Testament. Nashville: Thomas Nelson Publishers.

11. Merriam-Webster. (2015). Soul | Definition of Soul by Merriam-Webster. http://www.merriam-webster.com/dictionary/soul

12. Strong, J., & Strong, J. (1984). *The New Strong's Exhaustive Concordance of the Bible*: With main concordance, appendix to the main concordance, key verse comparison chart, dictionary of the Hebrew Bible, dictionary of the Greek Testament. Nashville: Thomas Nelson Publishers.

13. Merriam-Webster. (2015). Contain | Definition of Contain by Merriam-Webster. http://www.merriam-webster.com/dictionary/contain

14. Strong, J., & Strong, J. (1984). *The New Strong's Exhaustive Concordance of the Bible*: With main concordance, appendix to the main concordance, key verse comparison chart, dictionary of the Hebrew Bible, dictionary of the Greek Testament. Nashville: Thomas Nelson Publishers.

15. Strong, J., & Strong, J. (1984). *The New Strong's Exhaustive Concordance of the Bible*: With main concordance, appendix to the main concordance, key verse comparison chart, dictionary of the Hebrew Bible, dictionary of the Greek Testament. Nashville: Thomas Nelson Publishers.

16. BLB Institute. (n.d.). H905 - bad - Strong's Hebrew Lexicon (KJV). https://www.blueletterbible.org/lang/lexicon/lexicon.cfm?strongs=H905

17. Strong, J., & Strong, J. (1984). *The New Strong's Exhaustive Concordance of the Bible*: With main concordance, appendix to the main concordance, key verse comparison chart, dictionary of the Hebrew Bible, dictionary of the Greek Testament. Nashville: Thomas Nelson Publishers.

18. Strong, J., & Strong, J. (1984). *The New Strong's Exhaustive Concordance of the Bible*: With main concordance, appendix to the main concordance, key verse comparison chart, dictionary of the Hebrew Bible, dictionary of the Greek Testament. Nashville: Thomas Nelson Publishers.

19. BLB Institute. (n.d.). H5828 - `ezer - Strong's Hebrew Lexicon (NKJV). https://www.blueletterbible.org/lang/lexicon/lexicon.cfm?Strongs=H5828&t=NKJVdoes

20. BLB Institute. (n.d.). H5048 - neged - Strong's Hebrew Lexicon (KJV). https://www.blueletterbible.org/lang/lexicon/lexicon.cfm?t=kjv&strongs=h5048

21. Abbott, S. (2016, May 7). *What is a Helpmeet?* » Reasons for Hope* Jesus. https://reasonsforhopejesus.com/what-is-a-helpmeet/

22. Strong, J., & Strong, J. (1984). *The New Strong's Exhaustive Concordance of the Bible*: With main concordance, appendix to the main concordance, key verse comparison chart, dictionary of the Hebrew Bible, dictionary of the Greek Testament. Nashville: Thomas Nelson Publishers.

23. Leaf PhD, C. (2012, November 21). Blog | *Relationships: Man vs. Woman*. http://drleaf.com/blog/relationships-man-vs-woman/

24. Strong, J., & Strong, J. (1984). *The New Strong's Exhaustive Concordance of the Bible*: With main concordance, appendix to the main concordance, key verse comparison chart, dictionary of the Hebrew Bible, dictionary of the Greek Testament. Nashville: Thomas Nelson Publishers.

25. Merriam-Webster. (2015). Encompass | Definition of Encompass by Merriam-Webster. http://www.merriam-webster.com/dictionary/encompass

26. BibleHub. (2016). Jeremiah 31:22 Commentaries: "How long will you go here and there, O faithless daughter? For the LORD has created a new thing in the Earth-- A woman will encompass a man." http://biblehub.com/commentaries/jeremiah/31-22.htm

27.   Lytal, C. (2014, September 12). USC researchers discover the healing power of "rib tickling" I USC Stem Cell I USC. https://stemcell.usc.edu/2014/09/12/usc-researchers-discover-the-healing-power-of-rib-tickling/

28.   HeartMath Institute. (2015). https://www.heartmath.org/hmi/file/download.php?hma=xGdOHHK6PAcBPbINyTGHm1xetB5NKxEu Hm2Pt0be6TdciFlBIat3A2FHm1EbQHgF1A1c0gTp4skdjMQnszM0H m1SyJhUEw&hmaf=science-of-the-heart-vol-2.pdf&fh=view

29.   HeartMath Institute. (n.d.). Science of the Heart - HeartMath Institute. https://www.heartmath.org/research/science-of-the-heart/

30.   http://thinkexist.com/quotation/i-ve_learned_a_lot_about_women-i_think_i-ve/339357.html

31.   Strong, J., & Strong, J. (1984). *The New Strong's Exhaustive Concordance of the Bible*: With main concordance, appendix to the main concordance, key verse comparison chart, dictionary of the Hebrew Bible, dictionary of the Greek Testament. Nashville: Thomas Nelson Publishers.

32.   Cohen, L. *Anthem*. The Future. Sony/ATV Music Publishing LLC, 1992

33.   Myles, F. *The Order of Melchizedek, Tulsa: Word and Spirit Book*s. 2010. Page 152

34.   Eldredge, J. and S. *Captivating*. Nashville: Thomas Nelson, 2011 Print

35.   Myles, F. *The Order of Melchizedek Tulsa: Word and Spirit Books*. 2010. Page 159

36.   Tomlin, Chris. *You're a Good Good Father*, Never Lose Sight Album, Sparrow Records 2016.

37.   Eldredge, J. and S. *Captivating*. Nashville: Thomas Nelson, 2011 Print

38. Andrew Rader Studios. (1997). Physics4Kids.com: Electricity & Magnetism: Introduction. http://physics4kids.com/files/elec_intro.html

39. https:/heartmath.org/articles-of-the-heart/science-of-the-heart/the-energetic-heart-is-unfolding/

40. www.biblehub.com/hebrew/1288.htm. Strongs Hebrew; 1288 (barak) to Knell, Bless, BibleHub, 2004, Web, 12 September 2015

41. www.biblehub.com/hebrew/1397.htm, Strongs Hebrew; 1397 Warrior, BibleHub, 2004, Web, 12 September 2015

42. Niu, A. (2014, February 18). Gender & the Brain: Differences between Women & Men. http://www.fitbrains.com/blog/women-men-brains

43. Jantz PhD., G. (2014, February 27). *Brain Differences Between Genders* | Psychology Today. http://www.psychologytoday.com/blog/hope-relationships/201402/brain-differences-between-genders

44. Grant, B. (2013, December 4). *Male and Female Brains Wired Differently* | The Scientist Magazine®. http://www.the-scientist.com/?articles.view/articleNo/38539/title/Male-and-Female-Brains-Wired-Differently/

45. Sample, I. (2012, December 2). *Male and Female Brains Wired Differently, Scans Reveal* | Science | The Guardian. https://www.theguardian.com/science/2013/dec/02/men-women-brains-wired-differently